Wednesday's Child

Wednesday's Child

From Heidegger to Affective Neuroscience,
a Field Theory of *Angst*

GREGORY P. SCHULZ

WIPF & STOCK · Eugene, Oregon

WEDNESDAY'S CHILD
From Heidegger to Affective Neuroscience, a Field Theory of *Angst*

Copyright © 2011 Gregory P. Schulz. All rights reserved. Except for brief quotations in critical publications or reviews, no part of this book may be reproduced in any manner without prior written permission from the publisher. Write: Permissions, Wipf and Stock Publishers, 199 W. 8th Ave., Suite 3, Eugene, OR 97401.

Wipf & Stock
An Imprint of Wipf and Stock Publishers
199 W. 8th Ave., Suite 3
Eugene, OR 97401

www.wipfandstock.com

ISBN 13: 978-1-60899-684-1

Manufactured in the U.S.A.

For Paula

et inquietum est cor nostrum . . .

The trouble of the modern age is not merely the inability to believe certain things about God which our forefathers believed, but the inability to *feel* toward God and man as they did.

—T. S. Eliot, *On Poetry and Poets*, italics added

Contents

Foreword by Andrew Tallon / ix

Preface / xiii

ONE   From a Feeling of *Angst* to a Field Theory of Consciousness / 1
> *Introduction* / 1
> *To the Phenomenon Itself* / 1
> *An Implicit Field Theory* / 16
> *Summary* / 30

TWO   Toward an Affective Neuroscience of Mood / 34
> *Introduction* / 35
> *Affective Neuroscience-Plus* / 40
> *Beyond Basic Emotions and Anxiety Systems* / 50
> *Summary* / 60

THREE   How the Mood of *Angst* Might Be Verified Empirically / 62
> *Introduction* / 64
> *Environment as* Umwelt / 67
> *The Languages of Mind and Affective Neuroscience* / 72
> *The Background* / 76
> *Damasio at Solaris* / 81
> *Toward a Validation of* Angst *in the Common Language of Social Neuroscience* / 92
> *An Objection from Searle* / 102
> *Summary* / 112
> *Afterthought* / 114

Appendix: The Argument / 121

Glossary / 127

Bibliography / 131

Foreword

WHY DO WE CARE whether our feelings and moods are intentional? Why bother verifying what to most people seems an arcane question. Not everyone does care, of course. Philosophers ask such questions, and some psychologists and even some scientists, as least the neuroscientists who dialog with philosophers and psychologists. If not everyone cares, perhaps our question should be: Why *should* we care? One answer could be that if feelings and moods point to nothing, are *about* nothing, and go nowhere, then they are vain, epiphenomenal, superficial, and ultimately worthless passing mental events that we are just as well devaluing as minor aches and pains, as unimportant itches and twitches, as insignificant as fleeting thoughts and wishes, the temporarily distracting brain states that come and go but have no permanent meaning or value. But if our feelings and moods share status with our profoundest ideas and deepest desires and values, then they deserve our attention just as do the best of our ideas, those that direct human history, and as do those life-transforming commitments and decisions that we cherish as emerging from human freedom and self-determination. Are feeling and moods in that league?

Dr. Greg Schulz says they are, and he joins a solid but fairly young—as philosophical theories go—orientation that feelings, emotions, the high-level affective states, including those of longer duration like moods and quasi-permanent dispositions, are not just happenings inside our skulls, but are parts of a much larger field with physical and biological roots, that emerge in the full history of the evolution of the human species and in the individual evolutions of each human person from conception onward throughout life. And what Greg cares about most is the *social and ethical* fields that emerge when humans have constructed lives sharing not only cognition and volition but also affection. What we have in this dense book is a carefully sequenced presentation—one that will repay slow and patient study tolerant of expressions some of which are a bit difficult of access at first—of a coherent synthesis of distinct contributions to the thesis that affections reveal human existence as a general kind of being and as each one's individual life, just as helpfully and fundamentally as do our ideas and choices.

Why should we care? Because we need all the help we can get in the pursuit of meaning and value. Are we limited by our minds, by the history of human thought contained in all the lives and books? Or do we also have hearts? What about our feelings and passions, those affections that too much rational disdain shoves aside from the mainstream of solutions to the big questions? If our minds tell us that human existence is but sound and fury signifying nothing, could our hearts suggest otherwise? And of what import are our hearts if they do? What proof have we that what our hearts say about life and death, or love and hate, should merit our attention?

That is the question philosophers name the question about "whether affections are intentional," about whether they point beyond their mere occurrence "inside" consciousness to objective (not merely subjective) "outside" reality, to the real world of meanings, and to the real world of values. The best and strongest contemporary work on this question is being done in field theory, which is the study of meta-individual, interpersonal groupings or arrangements now recognized to be primary rather than secondary in the constitution of the individuals and persons that exist within their force and dynamic flow. Since philosophy began, ideas were unquestioned powers that moved people to voluntary acts that themselves drove history, while feelings and moods were deemed ephemeral affective sensations that were disparaged as interfering with the minds and wills of the great thinkers and movers, especially in matters ethical and political; medieval theories considered them lower animal passions, sensual remainders from a brutish past we were better to leave behind. Only for about a century have major philosophers taken affectivity seriously enough to lead to its integration into a triadic conception of consciousness, to an understanding of the "mind" in the broad sense of consciousness, as threefold, as "triune," in the term preferred by Paul MacLean in his pioneering *The Triune Brain in Evolution*. Triune consciousness maps onto the triune brain. But whereas the intentionality of two of the three kinds of consciousness was generally uncontested and therefore taken to locate us in the real world, the poor stepchild, our affective consciousness, was ignored or even maligned as not connected to outside reality at all, but said to report on an inside world of illusory emotions and moods. Does Wednesday's child describe life in everyone's world or only life in the world of this child of *Angst*?

Greg Schulz has here tried to answer this question using all the resources that have most recently become available while keeping his research accessible in a readable compass. He is well aware that he has really only opened a door rather than said the last word. No one ever has the last word, on this or on any perennial question that counts, on those questions that must drawn upon the best that the human, social, and physical sciences can contribute. What gives us hope that his opening will fare better than some others is that it moves out of the mind and into the social field, which is the only possible locus where intentionality can be tested given that the very meaning and value of any intentional consciousness, whether cognition, affection, or volition, is to work in the real world we share with others. What would we give for a kind of consciousness that revealed the world as it is, transcendent of wishful thinking and mere velleities? Is it Wednesday's child who holds the key, the key that opens that door?

Dr. Andrew Tallon
Professor of Philosophy
Marquette University

Preface

PHILOSOPHY OF EMOTION IS a vital topic within contemporary philosophy of mind. Just think of the work being done by Ronald de Sousa, Antonio Damasio, Paul Griffiths, and John Searle, to mention a few names. Beginning from insights latent in Heidegger's early philosophy, my argument is that, with the recognition of a suitable field of consciousness, it ought to be possible to speak scientifically about our noncognitional and nonvolitional but nevertheless rational moods, such as what Andrew Tallon in *Head and Heart* calls "that most celebrated mood," namely, *Angst*.

With the emergence of twentieth-century existentialism and its attention to human experience, and with Heidegger's revolutionary insight that an emotional mood such as *Angst* (long-term anxiety or anguish) has *intentionality*, the time was ripe for serious phenomenological work on the emotional aspect of our human being. Much more recently, advances in neurological imaging have enabled us to contemplate the phenomenon of human emotion scientifically. At present, the new discipline of social neuroscience affords us a philosophical and scientific opportunity to attend to the emotional aspect of our being, a long-neglected aspect of our humanity. Proceeding from Heidegger's insight regarding the intentionality of moods, this dissertation adumbrates a type of social neuroscience capable of validating Heidegger's understanding of the centrality of *Angst* for human being.

Wednesday's Child is a reworking of my PhD philosophy dissertation at Marquette University, Milwaukee. In particular, let me acknowledge the substantial contributions of Professor Anthony Peressini, whose contributions as a philosopher of mathematics and science were invaluable; and especially my director, Professor Andrew Tallon, whose courses in Aquinas and in Christian metaphysics and whose book, *Head and Heart*, initiated my philosophical interest in Heidegger and affectivity. Professor Javier Ibáñez-Noé encouraged my analysis of Heideggerian conscience and Professor Michael Vater taught me to be coherent in the development of my hypothesis.

ONE

From a Feeling of *Angst* to a Field Theory of Consciousness

> Clearly the anguish [running through the writings of the mystics] is that of separation and incompleteness at the level of existence. One can experience one's incompleteness emotionally or economically or culturally or sexually, and all this is painful. But how terrible to experience it at the deepest level of all, that of existence! For all these other sorrows are partial experiences of one root experience of existential contingency. And this, I believe, is the sorrow of the man who knows not only *what he is* but *that he is*. All this is not far removed from the anguish of the existentialist philosophers about which we at one time heard so much. Their agony was not necessarily theistic. Rather did it come from a radical sense of man's insufficiency, contingency, incompleteness, mortality, summed up in Heidegger's terrible definition of man as "being-to-death."
>
> —William Johnston, Introduction to *The Cloud of Unknowing*[1]

LET US UNDERTAKE A philosophical and scientific study of human anguish. Where shall we begin in order to find the phenomenon of *Angst* itself? The essence of anguish is disclosed, I submit to you, in Heidegger's existential analysis of conscience. For Heidegger, the mood of *Angst* is integral to our experience of conscience. Heidegger's existential analysis of conscience shows, in his characteristic vocabulary, that authentic *Dasein* (the interpreting human being, capable of deliberation) summons inauthentic *Dasein* to recognize in the very dissonance of the experience of *Angst* the potential to be a responsible self. *Angst* is thus itself a continual call to validate this dissonant feeling of insufficiency,

---

1. Johnston, *Cloud of Unknowing*, 10–11.

contingency, incompleteness, and mortality—that is, to ask whether our feeling points to anything real and objective or whether it is merely subjective. Can one be authentic and ignore this question? Heidegger points out how easy we find it to be to escape into "everydayness" (*Alltäglichkeit*) rather than deal with this question. It is easier to fall into the distraction of everyday living than face this call.

INTRODUCTION

The present study of *Angst* is not meant to serve as an historical rehearsal of an existentialist concept of which we used to hear a great deal. Nor is it meant to unpack Heidegger's "terrible definition" of man as being-to-death. Instead, I shall simply be arguing that, beginning from insights latent in Heidegger's phenomenological approach to human anguish, we today are in a position to verify our feeling of *Angst* in line with currently emerging neuroscience on the basis of the *intentionality* of this feeling, much as we are accustomed to verify the items of study in other scientific fields on the basis of the objectivity of those items. By "verify" I mean the understanding of empirical investigation such as we practice in the natural sciences. A related term, "validate," seems more appropriate for the way we used to speak in continental philosophy or phenomenology. Intentionality is objective in both manners of speaking. That is to say, moods have an object that is *validated* conceptually. In addition, moods have intentionality *and that their intentionality is an irreducible feature of moods* is a feature that can be verified objectively in terms of an appropriate contemporary neuroscience. First, though, we need to identify the phenomenon of our study, namely, anguish or *Angst*.

TO THE PHENOMENON ITSELF[2]

Somewhere between 1940 and 1943, at the monastery of Ettal and Kieckow, Martin Heidegger's countryman Dietrich Bonhoeffer wrote this about shame and conscience: "In shame man is reminded of his disunion with God and with other men: conscience is a sign of man's disunion with himself. Conscience is . . . the voice of apostate life which desires at least to remain one with self. It is the call to the unity of man with himself."[3] This is a remarkable understanding of conscience, philo-

---

2. See Schulz, "Non-Traditional Analysis of Conscience," 33–44.
3. Bonhoeffer, *Ethics*, 27–28.

sophically speaking. It is not Aquinas's understanding of conscience, nor is it Kant's. It is, however, a theological analog to the early Heidegger's philosophical presentation of conscience.

Philosophically, we are familiar with the notion that conscience is determined by its practical activity or content, as is the case with Aquinas and Kant, taking conscience to be a shared knowledge within human beings that establishes our moral obligations to God or to one another. But this is not at all what Bonhoeffer describes. He describes conscience as an indication of our essential disunity with ourselves and others in our world. This is the very same view of conscience elaborated by Martin Heidegger in *Being and Time*: "A more penetrating analysis of conscience reveals it as a *call* (*Ruf*). Calling is a mode of *discourse*. The call of conscience has the character of a *summoning Dasein* by calling it to its ownmost potentiality-of-being-a-self . . ."[4] What does this mean?

If conscience is such a call or summoning, this invites us to seek the answers to three basic questions. In the discourse of conscience:

1. Who is calling?
2. Who is being called?
3. To what is the listener being called?

In the course of answering these questions, we can conclude that Heidegger's understanding of conscience in *Being and Time* is unlike Aquinas's understanding of conscience as practical reason. It is furthermore unlike Kant's understanding of conscience as an internal courtroom. Both of these philosophical views of conscience exhibit a traditional way of considering conscience that Heidegger deliberately rejects or supersedes. Rather, for Heidegger, conscience constitutes a disclosure of *Dasein*'s existential anguish or *Angst* while being in the world. In this, conscience is a disclosure of the here-and-now, the *Da* of *Dasein*.

To put it another way, conscience discloses that, though the human being or *Dasein* is in the world, the human being is *unheimlich*, not at home with herself as being-in-the-world. One objection may be that conscience, inasmuch as it is a call involving oneself, presents a problem for the early Heidegger's phenomenological method (i.e., the

---

4. Heidegger, *Being and Time*, 269. The German pagination is indicated, unless otherwise noted.

method of *Being and Time*), namely, how to ground the existential presupposition that there exists, as a given, an ideal self to be appealed to. My argument, however, is to accept Heidegger's *existential* interpretation of conscience, entailing as it does our feeling of *Angst*, not as a way in itself for the human being to conduct herself ideally, but rather as the ground for the possibility of being a self or responsible human agent in the first place. An outcome of my argument is the recognition that, in terms of Heidegger's understanding of conscience, we can begin to see the phenomenon of our feeling of *Angst* for human being. A secondary outcome is the realization that *Angst*, when studied as the phenomenon it is, rather than as a notion conveniently downsized to fit a place in our theoretical commitments, exhibits *an intentionality that makes it not only reportable but also capable of validation.*

Who is calling? Authentic *Dasein* is calling. According to Heidegger, a human being is authentic insofar as she relates freely to the world in which she lives as herself. This is what is meant by *Dasein*'s "ownmost potentiality-of-being-a-self." Before explaining this more fully, it may help to set Heidegger's view of the caller against the understanding of two earlier philosophers as to who is calling via conscience. His philosophical precursors in this matter of "conscience" are Aquinas and Kant.

Heidegger differs from Aquinas in viewing conscience as a dialogue of self with self while being in the world contingently; Aquinas views conscience as the application of knowledge to a particular action. Aquinas sees conscience as moral activity resulting from the rational deliberation of practical reason. In the *Summa Theologiae*, he treats conscience under the heading of "Human Abilities—Bodily and Spiritual" in this way: "Conscience . . . is neither ability nor disposition, strictly speaking, but the activity of consciously applying our knowledge to what we do: witnessing to what we do and don't do, legislating about what we should and shouldn't do, and defending or accusing us when we have or haven't done well."[5] In Thomas' view, then, conscience is practical reasoning about moral matters.

For Heidegger, this traditional philosophical definition of conscience, which he calls the ordinary or "vulgar interpretation," needs to be replaced with an "existential interpretation:" "Our existential interpretation [of conscience] needs to be confirmed by a critique of the vul-

---

5. McDermott, *Summa Theologiae*, 124.

gar interpretation of conscience."[6] What Heidegger seeks in his critique of this ordinary interpretation of conscience is a more fundamental or existential basis for conscience. And so, Heidegger provides us with the supposition that conscience involves a bifurcation of the human being or *Dasein*. *Angst* is the megaphone alerting us to this fundamental schizophrenia. Da-sein is two-tiered. We can think of its makeup as being constituted of *Dasein* I and *Dasein* II.[7] In terms of what Heidegger refers to as the "thrown project," the human being is immersed in the world of common and public assumptions of its own being, the world of what Heidegger calls "they" or *das Man*. Immersed in the world of "they," the human being participates in worldly affairs and so finds significance. Call this *Dasein* I.

But the human being is uneasy and feels anxiety or *Angst* in this world of "they." This anxiety leads *Dasein* to realize that she has been thrown into a world that is not intrinsically satisfying. Call this *Dasein* II. *Dasein* II explains *Dasein* I inasmuch as the human being wants to fall back into the feeling of significance found from being immersed in worldly affairs such as "they" always are. *Dasein* I amounts to a noncognitive, nonreflective automatic assimilation into the anonymous, selfless, everyday routine of life. But then, as we can learn from the claxon of our feeling of *Angst*, *Dasein* II calls to *Dasein* I, so to speak, to get real, to be an individual, to be something more than *hoi poloi*, to be authentic and thus to come to grips with her own anguish. Now this call is not a call to action sounded by practical reason; it is rather a call of the self to the self. The thought of self calling self, insofar as it appears to be an autonomous notion of conscience, suggests that we next consider Kant's conception of conscience.

While in Thomas's view conscience is simply practical reasoning about moral matters, in Kant's view, conscience is an internal court within the rational human being. For Kant, as with Aquinas, conscience has to do with practical understanding. In his discussion of duty and conscience in *The Metaphysics of Morals*, Kant construes the concept of "duty" as a matter of an ongoing practical syllogism in which an individual, on the basis of her rationality, renders conclusions or verdicts while contemplating possible courses of action. Kant portrays conscience as a tribunal or *coram judicio* in which a moral person puts the law of reason

6. Heidegger, *Being and Time*, 269.
7. Inwood, *Heidegger Dictionary*, 37–39.

to work in an internal court or forum. In other words, the conclusions of practical reason are adjudicated within, in front of an internal tribunal, a personal court: "Consciousness of an *internal court* in the human being ('before which his thoughts accuse or excuse one another') is *conscience*."[8] Thus far Kant, with his metaphor of an internal courtroom, seems to view conscience in a manner similar to Heidegger's *Dasein* II summoning *Dasein* I. This presumed similarity with Heidegger is amplified by an extended footnote in which Kant explains that a "human being who accuses and judges himself in conscience must think of a dual personality in himself, a doubled self . . ."[9]

But the similarity to Heidegger is merely superficial. This becomes clear as Kant elucidates the parties involved in the courtroom of conscience. "Every human being has a conscience and finds himself observed, threatened and, in general, kept in awe (respect coupled with fear) by an internal judge."[10] The introduction of an internal judge or authority of some sort differentiates Kantian conscience from Heideggerian conscience in that Heidegger is concerned with the ground or basis of conscience as such. He sees conscience as a recognition, a deliberation, an understanding resulting from a fundamental disunity of one's self that is disclosed in our feeling of *Angst*. In marked contrast to Heidegger's critique, Kant concludes, "This authority watching over the law in him is not something that he himself (voluntarily) *makes*, but something incorporated into his being. It follows him like a shadow when he plans to escape."[11]

Kant indeed refers to this conscience as "a business of a human being with himself." He maintains in accordance with his plaintiff and defendant analogy that in conscience the human being "constrained by his reason sees himself constrained to carry on [the business of conscience, the internal court] as at the bidding *of another person*."[12] As it turns out, however, this other person is not oneself but an imagined or ideal other. Kant's "another person" is merely a quasi-person postulated within the internal courtroom for the purpose of ethical deliberation. In the aforementioned extended footnote to this section in *The Metaphysics*

8. Gregor, *Immanuel Kant*, 560.
9. Ibid., 560–61, footnote.
10. Ibid.
11. Ibid.
12. Ibid.

of Morals, Kant says, "A human being who accuses and judges himself in conscience must think of a dual personality in himself."

Here too Kant appears at a quick read to be speaking of conscience as Heidegger does, but this Kantian "dual personality" is a far cry from the *Dasein* I and *Dasein* II disclosed by our experience of *Angst* as identified by Heidegger. One of Kant's dual personalities, the judge, is clearly an ideal homunculus, a mere dialogic postulate. Such postulates are *apathetic* idealist constructions bereft of motivating force, but in his analysis of conscience, Heidegger clearly considers our feeling of *Angst* to be primordial, something that is inescapably there, a feature of the *Da* of *Dasein* before we ever set about the work of performing practical syllogistic calculations about the morality of contemplated actions.

The "vulgar" character of Kant's "ordinary interpretation" of conscience becomes readily apparent when we re-read Kant in light of the upcoming third question of conscience for Heidegger, the question as to what the listener is being called when the self calls the self in Heidegger's existential interpretation of conscience. Let me simply say at this point that Kant's conscience is hardly the existential self calling the self. In the Kantian conscience, another self is posited, to be sure. For Kantian conscience, the other self is another person or perhaps even the voice of God, in view of the parenthetical quotation of Paul's epistle to the Romans, but the other self is not really oneself and is not *Dasein*. It is also noteworthy that the Kantian call is a call to rationality and is thus, in a narrow etymological sense apathetic. A sure indication of this difference is Heidegger's well-known contention that *Dasein* experiences *Angst,* not as the consequence of its cognitive being, but inasmuch as *Dasein* has its being-toward-death. But before reaching the question as to what the listener is being called to, let us consider briefly to whom authentic *Dasein* is calling.

Who is being called? Everyday *Dasein* is being called. An everyday human being is a sort of generic everyman or hollow man, "cleansing affection from the temporal," a being of flickering attention and apathetic by default, but with the potential of being a genuine self. Left to itself in the midst of this they-to-they world, *Dasein* is a being "distracted from distraction by distraction," as T. S. Eliot has it.[13] The average hollow man is the type of human being Heidegger refers to as "they." In Division II of *Being and Time,* Heidegger begins to address this problem with what he

---

13. Eliot, *The Complete Poems and Plays,* 120.

calls an "Attestation of an Authentic Existentiell Possibility" concerning conscience and "the question of *the who of Da-sein*." In order to help us realize that we have the potential to extricate ourselves from "the they," Heidegger refers us to the familiar interpretation of our being human in terms of the voice of conscience.[14]

"As a phenomenon of *Dasein*, conscience is not a fact that occurs and is occasionally objectively present. It '*is*' only in the kind of being of *Dasein* and makes itself known as a fact only in factical existence."[15] This means that conscience is itself what we might call a brute existential fact, but for the fact that conscience and its concomitant feeling of *Angst* is, as Heidegger insists, a phenomenon that "is prior to any psychological description and classification of experiences of conscience, just as it lies outside any biological 'explanation'"[16] and ought therefore not to be depicted exclusively (or reductively) in a positivistic or scientific manner. Nor ought it to be regarded as the product of our psychology, as if conscience results from our willing and thinking. This does not, of course, make conscience somehow unreal. It is just that scientific methodologies, as "a physics of our mental life" that "presupposes a definition of the mind that is itself a definite transposition of a definite notion of the body,"[17] miss the phenomenon under study.

There is in conscience something to be understood, the insufficiencies of psychology and biology notwithstanding. "Conscience gives us 'something' to understand; it *discloses*."[18] Considering this phenomenologically, the facticity of conscience leads us back to the essential disclosedness of *Dasein*'s anxiety. In other words, attending to the phenomenon of conscience reveals the kind of being we human beings are. Conscience shows that we are the kind of beings who are constituted of mood, understanding, falling, and discourse. All in all, we are finite, anguished beings.

In the experience of a feeling such as *Angst*, we find ourselves enabled to understand that we are differentiated from the world of things and the faceless mass of "the they" in which we exist. Here, in Division II of *Being and Time*, we learn that conscience expresses the discourse that

14. Heidegger, *Being and Time*, 247–48.
15. Ibid.
16. Ibid., 269.
17. Taminiaux, *Metamorphoses of Phenomenological Reduction*, 11–12.
18. Heidegger, *Being and Time*, 269.

is constitutive of us as human beings or *Dasein*. On this analysis, conscience reveals mood, understanding, falling, and discourse to be "a *call* [*Ruf*]." "The call of conscience has the character of *summoning* Da-sein ..."[19] Think of it as a call to our unique vocation of being. Our question at this point is: a summoning to whom? We have established that authentic *Dasein*, or *Dasein* II, is making the appeal. Can we now say with more specificity who is being called or summoned?

Specifically, authentic *Dasein* is calling to inauthentic *Dasein*. Recall that the summons is to *Dasein*'s "ownmost potentiality-of-being-a-self." Let us continue to take "inauthentic *Dasein*" to be *Dasein* I. *Dasein* I is the human being under the sway of "the they." This inauthentic *Dasein* is being called to awaken to its potential to step away from easy and automatic anonymity in order to become a self. The human being is being called to be all that a human being can be. Here is where Heidegger seeks to debunk what he calls "the ordinary theory of conscience" for which my examples have been Aquinas and Kant, according to his "existential interpretation."

The linchpin for the existential interpretation of conscience lies right here: "To the call of conscience there corresponds a possible hearing. Understanding the summons reveals itself as *wanting to have a conscience* [*Gewissenhabenwollen*]."[20] Yes, but why? How can this summons be a call? How can a state of affairs move us? It has to do with the irrefragable phenomenon of *Angst*. One way of expressing this concern would be to ask how real in the sense of how persistent and how beyond our cognitive control this summons to authenticity is as a call to inauthentic *Dasein* to be authentic.

Essentially, this clarion call to authenticity never ceases, though it is not generally heeded. The call is a *mood*. It is not an occasionally reiterated call directed to inauthentic *Dasein* as such, but it is constitutive of *Dasein*'s being inasmuch as Heidegger's existential interpretation of conscience accounts for the *Da* of *Dasein*. Attuned to our anxiety, we as *Dasein* can know where we stand in the world but tend thoughtlessly to keep our fingers over our ears and drown out the voice of our self calling our self in the anxious dialogue of conscience,[21] thus losing ourselves in the "publicness of the they" and its "idle talk." In the experience of

19. Ibid.
20. Ibid.
21. Ibid., 281.

conscience provoked by *Angst*, we can understand our potential, if only we have ears to hear. "To the call of conscience there corresponds a possible hearing."[22] *Dasein* is *Dasein*, but the human being comes to understand herself *as* a human being by virtue of this *Angst*-ridden oscillation between authentic self and inauthentic self. The problem, as I have said, is not the intermittent character of the call but the inattentiveness of *Dasein* and the white noise of "the they."

Think of it as a philosophical analog to Luther's *simul justus et peccator*. The authentic viewpoint is of oneself as a being free to be a project, to be detached from the common, self-interested attachments to the things of this world. The inauthentic viewpoint is of oneself as attached self-interestedly to the things of this world, to other beings. But even if one is living inauthentically at the level of Da-sein I, one is nevertheless Da*sein*, an existing being who has the potential to know oneself as being different from other beings by virtue of one's finitude. This differentiatedness is disclosed or attested to by the activity of conscience, the self calling the self. And as Heidegger insists, the activity of conscience is not intermittent. "As a phenomenon of *Dasein*, conscience is not a fact that occurs and is only occasionally present,"[23] as we have noted. The summoning is incessant for the human being as *Dasein*. The calling is unremitting, though not always listened to resolutely.

Thus we begin to recognize that in this incessant appeal "something" is being given to us to understand. The "something" given in this primordial summoning is the validation of our own unique being or Da*sein*. And so, existing here and now as *Dasein*, we want to ask whether in this existential phenomenon of conscience the authentic self is calling the inauthentic self to "something" that we can articulate.

To what is the listener being called? Authentic *Dasein* is calling everyday *Dasein* "to 'something.'" *Dasein* is being called to historical being (i.e., to realize its capability of being a self engaged with the world). But the question arises as to how, and on what basis. In a word, what does this call intend?

In Section 56, "The Character of Conscience as a Call," Heidegger explains that in the call of conscience what occurs is a movement in which authentic *Dasein* effectively passes over the public persona of the human being (which Heidegger calls "the they") in order to summon

22. Ibid., 269–70.
23. Ibid.

oneself to be a genuine self. "And to what is one summoned? To one's *own self*."²⁴ Now the worry that arises here is that conscience may be a summoning oneself to oneself merely monologically, leaving us to subsist as Kant's "wretched I." It may seem that Heidegger's is an incorrigibly egotistical view of conscience. But for Heidegger, the self is always being-in-the-world, never the radically individualized self of Kant's philosophy. Further, our being is always considered with a view toward our own death and finitude. In this way, instead of becoming wretchedly and radically untethered selves, we realize that we exist *here and now* as *In-der-Welt-sein*. According to Division I, we are historical beings in this sense, as being-to-death.

By the time we reach Division II, however, the worry about the who of *Dasein*, whether "I" am a genuine historical person in and of myself, or a miserable egotist,²⁵ has been parsed into the two selves of conscience. There is a call to self here in this latter portion of *Being and Time*, but it now develops that it would be premature to take this as a call to historical being *simpliciter*, inasmuch as Heidegger holds not the ordinary but an *existential* interpretation of conscience.

An objection to this strong existential view of conscience may be raised in view of Heidegger's linkage between conscience and guilt. Indeed, this seems to push his notion of conscience back toward the ordinary, vulgar interpretation of conscience. "Guilt" seems to presuppose the presence of an ideal self. But this is not the case. In fact, Heidegger's understanding of guilt is similarly existential and unconditional as such. "In the message delivered in the call [of conscience] the ordinary Da-sein is told about its own guilt. But while Da-sein, as the addressee and the bearer of this message of guilt, is indeed the ordinary Da-sein, the guilt . . . addressed to ordinary Da-sein is general and unconditional . . . the call of conscience tells me I am guilty insofar as I (merely) am."²⁶ Heideggerian guilt is not liability to punishment, as the ordinary interpretation of "guilt" would run; rather significantly, it is the unsettled feeling of being human.

The call of conscience is a call that identifies human beings *as* human beings to themselves. Such a call of conscience when considered religiously will terminate in a revelation, an encounter with the divine,

24. Ibid., 273.
25. Ibid., 109 (English pagination). See Stambaugh's footnote.
26. Hoffmann, "Death, Time, History," 210–11.

if the human being is to see herself as being in the world yet not of it. But the call itself, on the existential interpretation of conscience, is antecedent to any revelation. This point has been a difficult one even for Heidegger commentators to articulate within the common conversation, as if Heidegger were proceeding in his analysis essentially apart from the theological tradition and a more scientific study of conscience.

As a case in point, Magda King seems to imply that Heidegger's notion of conscience is *de nova*. She appears to exempt the existential from conceptions of the ordinary interpretation of conscience when she tells us, "The existential interpretation of conscience will, of course, be unacceptable not only to the scientific, but even more to the theological explanations of the same phenomenon."[27] But theological or scientific explanations of conscience operate at the level of the ordinary view of conscience. They assume the ordinary interpretation of conscience as the object of their belief or knowledge. Heidegger's is not the ordinary interpretation; his analysis of conscience is an existential analysis. We could say that Heidegger's existential interpretation is foundational for the traditional theological or scientific and psychological understanding of conscience. This makes his analysis of conscience, entailing as it does the mood of *Angst* of interest to theologians and scientists alike.

Heidegger is, of course, markedly nontheistic in his analysis of conscience, but this is not the same thing as being anti-theological nor, by the way, as being antiscientific, strictly speaking. Rather, his is a view of conscience before it can be amenable to scientific or theological analysis. The Heideggerian conscience, inasmuch as it is an existential concept, is prior to any theological or scientific account. In the same way and for the same reason, *Angst* is an *a priori* or primordial phenomenon of being human beings that simultaneously precedes any and every interpretation of its object. What we seek, then, is an understanding of the source or cause of *Angst*. If *Angst* is intentional, then its source is the thing it is *about*. On the other hand, if *Angst* is nonintentional, then its source is not what the mood is about. Rather, its source is what causes or determines our anxiety. Either way, one may look for the source in order to validate this feeling. In the intentional case, what validates *Angst* is that it is about the right thing or about something at all. However, in the nonintentional case, what validates the feeling is that it is caused by the right thing and is caused in the right way. This is similar to validating a

---

27. King, "Witness to an Owned Existence," 167.

coin, which amounts to ascertaining that it was caused in the right way, namely by the appropriate minting agency. In this latter case, we can have validation without intentionality.

So, without recourse to revelation, we want to see where this philosophical analysis of conscience gets us. This leads us to a *fundamental* concern, one recognized by Heidegger in *Being and Time*: what is the ground of the presupposition of an ideal self such as recurs in the traditional interpretation of conscience, by which "the they" regularly endeavor to make us less anguished about our human *Angst*?

Let us grant, in sympathy with the commonly acknowledged morality of the traditional, ordinary interpretation of conscience, that being without doing, like faith without works, is dead. Such a stipulation will entail a discussion of moral ideals: wanting to be a person of a certain sort, such as Socrates or Saint Paul or Joan of Arc. Thinking thus sympathetically, we may be tempted to scour *Being and Time* for such exemplars of heroic *Dasein*, but there are none to be found. Heidegger's point is that *Dasein* has the *freedom* to choose its ideal, but Heidegger does not intend his analysis of conscience to deliver the ideal per se, but rather the conditions under which *Dasein* can and does choose whatever it chooses. "[T]he possibility that Da-sein may choose its hero—is grounded existentially in anticipatory resoluteness."[28]

Frustrated in our search for ideal human being, we may look within for indications of an innate ideal *Dasein*, but in vain. In terms of the project of *Being and Time*, this frustration is itself instructive. How is it that we are frustrated? What is the cash value of our anxiety? Can we somehow conclude that the feeling of *Angst* has worth for understanding ourselves and even undertaking our moral projects?

For Heidegger, our human being is constituted by inner dialogue with itself, *Dasein* in dialogue with *Dasein*. Yet this is never a dialogue within a Cartesian theater. *Dasein* understands whatever it understands, including especially itself, in relation to itself as being-in-the-world. But this self-understanding is hardly sedate and cognitively comfortable. On the contrary, it is unsettled and anxious. Our self-understanding is not a completed project to be shelved and filed away. It is a constant project, as Heidegger says, driven by our feeling *Angst*. Contra Aristotle, philosophy does not begin in wonder; it begins in anguish. This is how we know that we know what the possibilities of existence are, as human beings

---

28. Heidegger, *Being and Time*, 385.

who contemplate the "what-ifs" of our actual choices in our world. Our innermost self is essentially this perpetual discussion of what we should be. Our own being is constantly at issue. This is what we know existentially and perhaps even pragmatically and unavoidably in the fact of conscience, the self calling the self resolutely.[29] This perturbation, this *Angst*, is proto-ethical. That is to say, our not being at home with ourselves in the world is the ground of our moral being, the basis on which the very possibility of normative action rests.

Now the calling of *Dasein* to *Dasein* is *resolute*, unremitting, part and parcel of our being human. This ontic, temporal fact, though allowed in the ordinary nonexistential interpretation, is there assumed, without being fully investigated. Indeed, the ordinary interpretation of conscience itself depends upon what Heidegger might call this "more primordial" grasp of the phenomenon. The ordinary interpretation of conscience would seem to invite a further investigation into this internal dialogue, in the sense that conscience cannot be said to do *moral* work unless it is unequivocally grounded in the being of the moral agent, the human being, *Dasein*.

And so, there is a more modest and primordial, and simultaneously a more existential, understanding of the place of conscience presented to us in *Being and Time*. In the disquieted calling or inner dialogue of conscience, *Dasein* understands that it is, amid the muddle of the world, already engaged in interpretation (*Auslegung*), a "self understanding of understanding."[30] On this possibility or foundation of becoming itself in the ongoing activity of understanding[31] the human being is open to being an historic, morally interactive self. This openness is not the historical self, that is to say, the self engaged with society or other human beings, nor is it the authentic self per se; it is more properly the ground for the possibility of the historical self. In order to be an historical self participating authentically in the activities of life, whether momentous or mundane, one must know oneself, anxiously, as an authentic self.

Now, this historical self may be established via divine revelation. As Bonhoeffer the theologian has it: "Conscience comes from a depth which lies beyond a man's own will and his own reason and it makes itself heard as the call of human existence to unity with itself . . . the great change comes at the moment when the unity of human existence ceases

---

29. Grondin, "The Ethical and Young Hegelian Motives," 348.
30. Ibid.
31. See, for example, Heidegger, *Being and Time*, 148ff.

to consist in its autonomy and is found, through the miracle of faith, beyond the man's own ego and its law, in Jesus Christ."[32] Or this historical self may be established on the basis of poetry as revelation, as the later Heidegger has it: "In poetry man is reunited on the foundation of his own existence. There he comes to rest; not indeed to the seeming rest of inactivity and emptiness of thought, but to that infinite state of rest in which all powers and relations are active."[33] But either way, Heidegger tells us, the possibility of becoming an historical self is founded on the existing self as such coming into her own. To be precise, the possibility of becoming an historic self—a "moral self" we could just as well say—is founded on the existential mood of *Angst*, which is constitutive of the human being and is understood originally in the ongoing fact of existential conscience, self calling self resolutely, all the while in-the-world.

To summarize my analysis to this point: our investigation into the place of conscience in Heidegger's *Being and Time* has provided a view of conscience that is *existential* and therefore critical of the ordinary interpretation in the sense that it investigates and discloses the ground or basis on which the ordinary interpretation depends. The ordinary interpretation, as seen in Aquinas's *Summa Theologiae* and in Kant's *The Metaphysics of Morals*, is that conscience, an exercise of practical reason, serves to differentiate moral from immoral actions. By contrast, Heidegger's existential interpretation teaches us to acknowledge our human *Angst* and come thus to view conscience as the ground for the possibility of moral differentiation. Conscience, an inner dialogue of the authentic self calling to the inauthentic self while being-in-the-world, serves in this view as an incessant agitation. Conscience gives us "'something' to understand" even when we are immersed in the common world of "the they." However, only when we are attentive to *Angst* as a primordial feeling or mood as it is identified in Heidegger's existential analysis of conscience do we begin to understand the worth of *Angst*. This "something" of which Heidegger speaks is what we come to know of ourselves, not in terms of psychology or biology, but in terms of "conscience" where we recognize our feeling of *Angst* for what it always is: a fundamental and inescapable anxiousness to seek to become at home with our own being, somehow.

---

32. Bonhoeffer, *Ethics*, 238–39.
33. Quoted in Brock, *Martin Heidegger*, 286.

With the phenomenon of *Angst* in view, let us turn next to a more particular study of *Angst* as a mood (i.e., as a more specific term for feeling and affection). With Heidegger's existential analysis of conscience in mind, we are in a position to consider the intentionality of *Angst* and thus begin to see how we are able not only to *describe* a feeling such as *Angst* but to *validate* it phenomenologically and are furthermore able to verify it in a suitable neuroscientific manner.

AN IMPLICIT FIELD THEORY

Heidegger defines feeling as "the way we find ourselves in relationship to beings, and thereby at the same time to ourselves." [34] This is at least an implicit, abbreviated field theory of consciousness. A generation ago, Bernard Lonergan argued for the scientific worth of what he called "the subjective field of common sense."[35] Such a subjective field or pattern of experience that takes account of human subjects in the world in terms of their patterns of experience perceptually, biologically, aesthetically, and intellectually over time—not as relations of things to other things, but as conscious beings relating to one another in a shared environment. It is important, as we shall see, that the phenomenon of *Angst* is not itself confined to the region of biology or of intellect but is best studied in terms of the entire conscious field. Only in this way can we be methodologically careful not to reduce the phenomenon as it is to a preconception as we may wish it to be.

Angst is not reducible to human cognition or to human volition. Rather, as a feeling or mood, *Angst* discloses being to consciousness, and as a mood, it is thus as fundamental to our self-understanding as are our cognitive and volitional faculties. It is fundamental to how we know ourselves as human beings, namely, already or immediately in-the-world, in this field of consciousness or pattern shared with other conscious beings. *Angst* is thus intentional, just as cognition is. That is to say, *Angst* brings an aspect of our human nature to consciousness, thereby allowing us to contemplate our finite or mortal being in a fully human mode or mood. In order to see that this is so, we need to cast our net a bit more broadly to consider that feelings, emotions, or moods are amenable to scientific study, though not necessarily to hasty or what Heidegger calls "immedi-

---

34. Heidegger, "Will as Affect, Passion, and Feeling," 51.
35. Lonergan, *Insight*, 181–206.

ate" scientific classifications. This calls for a cautionary philosophical tale regarding theorizing about emotions.

Which modern philosopher is least likely to provide a validating analysis of the phenomena of our emotional feelings, our feeling *Angst*, or of conscience? The answer is Nietzsche. In *Nietzsche: An Introduction to the Understanding of His Philosophical Activity* Karl Jaspers writes, "Wherever Nietzsche does speak of love . . . he fails to illumine it as a personally experienced source. . . . There is no place for anxiety and conscience, inescapably so since Nietzsche denies their truth and value."[36] This denial of the truth and value of *Angst* results, according to Jaspers, from Nietzsche's propensity to speak "out of his states," leaving any reader who has not already unconsciously entered the states in which Nietzsche thinks his thoughts unable to make sense of Nietzsche. "That is why it is obvious that the states implied by Nietzsche could not be mere moods or experiences. They are rather . . . life-governing impulses: within them and through their movement *Existenz* becomes conscious of itself and its being."[37] Such "life-governing impulses" or instincts are readily reducible to biological explanations and psychological descriptions and can thus be disregarded as a valid dimension of human life; whereas moods, according to my hypothesis, are beyond biological explanations and psychological description and thus cannot be offhandedly diminished and dismissed. As Jaspers observes, "The germ of this misunderstanding is in Nietzsche himself."[38] Thus Nietzsche's misunderstanding invites us to pursue the question, "What, if anything, are our moods *about*?"

I have begun to argue that our feeling of *Angst* exhibits intentionality. This is, in essence, to disagree fundamentally with *Angst* as analyzed in the existential tradition, with the exception of Heidegger. Existentialists tend to write as if moods such as *Angst* are *about* the individual, herself by herself, period. For example, when Jaspers speaks of Nietzsche's propensity to speak "out of his states," this is another way of saying that moods lack intentionality on Nietzsche's account. In order to persuade us of any validity of emotions, much less moods, Nietzsche has to play the Pied Piper and conduct us into his own frame of mind. By means of the enthralling power of his words and through the Dionysian rhythms of his drunken songs and incantations of eternal recurrence, he must lead

36. Jaspers, *Nietsche*, 348.
37. Ibid., 339.
38. Ibid.

us to become intoxicated ourselves and thus to enter within his mood, or he has nothing more to say. Things are similar for other existentialist thinkers, for whom *angoisse* (Sartre), *Angst um das eigentliche Sein als Existenz* (Jaspers), and *angest* (Kierkeggard) are about anxiety for one's own individual existence.[39] In the philosophies of these thinkers, *Angst* is about oneself, with only incidental engagement with the world, at best. It is otherwise with Heidegger.

In order to inoculate our understanding of *Angst* and mood against Nietzschean (and existential) subjectivity, Heidegger elaborates an intentionality of feeling in the course of his Nietzsche lectures. On the basis of Heidegger's definition of "a feeling" or *Gefühl* in these lectures as "the way we find ourselves in relationship to beings, and thereby at the same time to ourselves,"[40] we acquire a philosophical resistance to dissolutions or scientific reductions of any sort that would strip the phenomenon of *Angst* of its intentionality, and at the same time, we come to appreciate the revelatory value of this phenomenon as what we may call "a normative datum" for coming to know ourselves as human beings always engaged with our world. But our understanding of this phenomenon—not the phenomenon itself, in fact, but our apprehension of *Angst*'s intentionality—depends in the first place upon our recognition of emotional and moody intentionality.

Let me stipulate that "cognition" in this connection means "any kind of mental operation or structure that can be studied in precise terms."[41] I do not include in cognition, even in "unconscious cognition," the operations or structure that are sometimes referred to as "basic emotions" or feelings inasmuch as I take our feeling of *Angst*, for example, to be a datum *for* cognition but not reducible *to* cognition. The modest conclusion of my analysis of *Angst* is not that affections are better than cognition in guiding action or that emotions and moods compete with cognitions in affecting decisions, but that affections deserve a place at the table instead of being methodically excluded in theory from ethical and other choices. It could be said, in fact, that my thesis endeavors to validate in

---

39. For a taxonomy of *Angst* and intentionality among existential thinkers, see Smith, *The Felt Meanings of the World*, 134–46.

40. Heidegger, "Will as Affect, Passion, and Feeling," 51.

41. Lakoff and Johnson, *Philosophy in the Flesh*, 11. For their fuller preliminary discussion of cognition, including unconscious cognition, see "The Cognitive Unconscious," 9–15.

theory what is already the case in *practice*—namely, that moods, in the best sense of the term, are a dimension of a full and integral human life, of human being, of *Lebensform*. As mentioned, this validation hinges on the intentionality of our moods.

Intentionality is a familiar notion, but its application to emotional theory has not yet been worked out. John Searle's definition of intentionality in his 1983 book of that same title is a case in point. "Intentionality," Searle explains, "is that property of many mental states and events by which they are directed at or about or of objects and states of affairs in the world."[42] Searle elaborates on his understanding of intentionality by arguing that if a mental state is intentional, then there must be an answer to the question as to what that mental state is *about*. In considering the putative intentionality of anxiety, Searle is at pains to point out that intentionality is not the *aboutness* of conscious experience. That is, although I may be conscious *of* my feeling of anxiety, this is not the same as what the feeling itself is about. His concept of intentionality is thus unabashedly scientific in that it invites us to investigate not whether we are conscious of our feelings and other mental states—in other words, to undertake a kind of spring cleaning of the furniture within our minds—but whether our mental states are *about* anything, objectively speaking. In point of fact, Searle denies intentionality to *Angst*, if, that is, I am correct in identifying *Angst* with what he refers to as "undirected anxiety:" "Undirected anxiety, depression, and elation are not Intentional, the directed cases are Intentional."[43]

By means of Searle's differentiation between undirected and directed cases of anxiety, I take it that, if I am anxious about your acceptance of my argument in this book, Searle would acknowledge the intentionality of my anxiety, whereas if I am anguished about my temporary relationship to the world as a whole, he would deny the intentionality of my *Angst*. While accepting his overall notion of intentionality, including the validation of a feeling of anxiety, for example, on the basis of its objectively discernible object, I will nevertheless take issue with Searle's restrictive notion as to what may constitute an intentional object. So as not to sound as if I am seeking to overwrite Searlean intentionality with a less-than-objective, alleged intentionality of an entirely different sort, I shall refer to the *quasi*-intentionality of our mood of *Angst*. By do-

42. Searle, *Intentionality*, 1.
43. Ibid., 2.

ing this, I do not mean to disavow Searle's argument for intentionality. Rather, I mean to argue that there is no warrant here for excluding the world as a whole as the object that *Angst* as a mood can be *about*.

Recall Heidegger's observation, in his Nietzsche lecture, that a feeling is an essential openness to … what? It is "the way we find ourselves in relationship to beings, and thereby at the same time to ourselves."[44] It is an openness to our ontological habitat,[45] to our own being and the being of others. Let me first say a bit more about the structural character of this openness and then proceed to explain how the validity of *Angst* can be established on the basis of its quasi-intentionality.

It is easy to misconstrue Heidegger's concept of openness and as a consequence, minimize the worth of the abbreviated conscious field theory implicit in Heideggerian *Angst*. We tend to construe the human being on the model of Russian dolls, with conscious selves nested within material selves, with the "real selves" thus placed at one remove from their extra-mental environment and subject to the reliable mediation of their *cognitive* abilities in order to know about the world.

Such presuppositions mask the already-in-the-world structure of Heidegger's understanding of the human being—not as an allegedly solitary mental being, naturally skeptical that thoughts or feelings can ever be intentional, but as being-in-the-world to begin with. Heidegger suggests a paradigmatic alternative that may be of use for our more scientific consideration of this mood. Heidegger's *Angst* is not about *my* (inner) existence. Rather, *Angst* is about being-in-the-world as such.[46] Heidegger is quite clear in speaking of what he calls the "structural concretion" of his investigation into the formal concept of *Dasein* that the determinations of *Dasein*'s being must be seen and understood as being grounded *a priori* upon being-in-the-world.[47] It is on the recognition of this pre-existing structure that we are in a position to apprehend the quasi-intentionality of *Angst* in this way: anxiety is not about objects or events in this world in the restrictive manner suggested by Searle; indeed, as Heidegger says, "What *Angst* is about is not an innerworldly

---

44. Heidegger, "Will as Affect, Passion, and Feeling," 51.
45. See Smith, *Felt Meanings of the World*, 144.
46. This is adapted from *Felt Meaning of the World*, 144–45.
47. Heidegger, *Being and Time*, 53.

being.... What *Angst* is about is completely indefinite."[48] This is not the same thing as saying that *Angst* is not about anything, of course.

Inasmuch as *Angst* is a feeling about something, even something indefinite, it exhibits intentionality in the manner I have mentioned, suggesting that this mood may be conceptually validated and perhaps even empirically verified by pursuing the question, "What is it about (as it must be *about* something in order to be intentional) and, in addition, is it *about* the right thing?" I have labeled this a quasi-intentionality in order to avoid the potential misunderstanding that anxiety is about innerworldly objects. For similar reasons, I require terminology that will allow us to articulate an intentionality that is indeed objective, but not in the narrow, assumed sense that the only object that a mental state can be about must be a defined object or would be definable in principle as an innerworldly object. In familiar Continental vocabulary, I shall refer to the completely indefinite, quasi-intentional object of our mood of *Angst* in terms of the "horizons" that it brings to consciousness. With this discussion of the horizons as the objects at which a mood aims, I mean to show that our human experience of moods can be described in a preliminary way as objective and valid in what we may call a secondary manner. This is so because moods aim at nonobjects that are the conditions for the presentation of objects. That is to say, again, that moods are in fact intentional *as moods* and not, in some piggyback fashion, intentional only as cognitions of definite objects. I take Searle to be correct when he maintains that Intentionality (his capitalization) pertains only to innerworldly objects when we are speaking of cognitive intentionality. Cognition requires intelligible objects as a condition of intentionality, well and good. However, moods are not cognitions. Moods do not require intelligible objects as a condition of intentionality; rather, they link to nonobjects or what we may acknowledge as the background wherein we identify objects as the targets of intentionalities. Moods aim at these horizons that are given nonobjectively when objects are given.

The linchpin for this step in my argument is to show that a mood—in the case of this study, the chief example offered by Heidegger, *Angst*—aims at horizons and thereby opens up further horizons. To put this another way: a mood's nonobjective given-ness, while it may seem at first to rule out any possibility of validating the feeling (as is argued in my third chapter below by one objector), does not at all disqualify

48. Ibid., 186.

a mood such as *Angst* from scientific investigation. This is so because moods can move to the forefront of attention when a deeper horizon is projected. This horizonal openness is analogous to a family on vacation. Their trip is, say, west to the Rocky Mountains. As they travel along, the edge of the mountain range looms and that, explains Dad, is what they are headed for. Gradually, the first mountain distinguishes itself and that, Mom says, is what they are headed for. One mountain opens to another for the family. The mountains open up the coastlands, the coastlands the Pacific Ocean, and perhaps, a sunset into the Pacific Ocean opens up the solar system to them all. One horizon brought into plain sight brings another. The ontological landscape opens to us in a similar fashion. Provided, that is, that we do not put our hands over our eyes or stick our fingers in our ears in order to avoid the journey altogether. As we can sense in Heidegger's existential analysis of conscience and the phenomenon of the mood of anguish, we ought naturally to seek to understand what the mood discloses, that is what it is about, its intentionality.

Validating a mood in a more scientific fashion than Heidegger did, which is to say *verifying* a mood empirically, is a more promising undertaking today than it would have been even a decade ago. The current status of the question as to whether and how emotions and moods can be validated (i.e., shown to be objective and intentional) depends upon recent discoveries in the field of neuroscience that indicate the obsolescence of philosophies of mind that equate our minds with our brains or even our minds with our brain-and-body organisms, but in place of these models appear to demand a field theory of consciousness in which mind is best construed as brain-plus-body-plus-world. Here we find ourselves, in the discourse of the latest neuroscience, arguing on scientific grounds for a field theory such as the theory implicit in Heidegger's ontology of being-in-the-world. But neither Heidegger nor Wittgenstein (whom I shall cite as well) ought to be regarded as oracles who can do no wrong, of course. Their insights into moods and field of behavior call for scientific verification in turn. Accordingly, the application of this field theory to our study of *Angst* is the topic of the following two chapters. In the course of these chapters, I shall borrow from these two philosophers those aspects of their work that may be taken to further my thesis that a mood such as *Angst* is amenable to verification in social neuroscience.

As to the link with the horizons, the coherence of mood's intentionality is the immediacy and unbidden character of our feelings or emotions that differentiate our emotions qualitatively from our ideas and our ratiocinations. It would seem that we ought to be able, on an open-minded and yet suitably scientific reading of these philosophers writing on the intentionality of moods (Heidegger) and the way in which feelings can be understood within a suitably verifiable background (Wittgenstein), to validate the moody ties that open up, so to speak, the horizons of our being-in-the-world.

On a less-significant level, we may find that this is as well an occasion for scientific self-criticism for those of us who theorize about emotion. The lesson is the same for twenty-first century theories of emotional feeling as it was for Nietzsche's nineteenth-century theories of will to power or eternal recurrence: "The one fundamental point to realize here is that no result of any science can ever be applied *immediately* to philosophy," Heidegger cautions. How, then, can we develop a philosophy of feeling that takes proper account of *Angst* as it is, with due regard for its intentionality, for its emotional objectivity?

In our Nietzsche lecture, Heidegger follows up his caution against the uncritical *immediate* acceptance of science for philosophical work with an exercise in attention to what he regards as "keensighted" "popular speech"[49] in order to disclose precisely what we can learn about "affect" and "passion" in order to understand "feeling." Heidegger writes, "Anger, for instance, is an affect. In contrast, by 'hate' we mean something quite different. Hate is not simply another affect, it is not an affect at all. It is a passion. But we call both of them 'feelings.'"[50] Heidegger explains that anger, as an ecstatic state, affects our being powerfully, or as Nietzsche has it, is "will to power." This powerful, momentary affect can be differentiated from a long-term passion such as hate, but affects and passions are alike in that they are an unavoidable aspect of our very way of being.

In part this is the case because emotions and moods are, as Robert Solomon and Martha Nussbaum have recently been arguing, intelligent. But contra their argumentational strategies, I do not agree that emotions are intelligent inasmuch as they are essentially cognitive. Affects such as anger and passions such as hate disclose, in Heidegger's language, the grip that being has on us "even when we are unwilling. That genuine willing which surges forward in resoluteness, that 'yes,' is what instigates

---

49. Heidegger, "Will as Affect, Passion, and Feeling," 46.
50. Ibid., 45.

the seizure of our entire being, of the very essence within us."[51] *Dasein* as being-in-the-world entails access to being, our own being and the being of others. *Dasein*, we must note carefully, *feels* but is not the fountainhead of its feelings; certainly it does not produce feelings by conscious or unconscious cognition. Feeling is categorically unlike ideas or thoughts in this respect.

Our feelings are undeniably a personal, existential aspect of our being human beings, but not exclusively of our individual humanity in abstraction from our social interaction with others. Our feelings are natural features of our being in nature. Our feelings do not come upon us from the outside, nor is it correct to say that they are explainable as mere mental states (recall here the intentionality of emotions and moods) inasmuch as they are already part and parcel of our kind of being. There is here no inner-outer divide. But feelings do determine how we see the world and thus how we relate to the world *apart from our thinking or our willing*. Far better to analyze our feelings, then, as "conscious connaturality" or as pre-cognitive resonances[52] inasmuch as we *feel* by virtue of our natural kind of being, rather than as outcomes we reach as the result of rational calculation or as products resulting from our deliberative willing.

Further on in his Nietzsche lecture, Heidegger defines affect as "the seizure that blindly agitates us" and passion as "the lucidly gathering grip on beings."[53] He then goes on to conclude that, beyond the existential flare-ups of affects such as anger, our long-lasting passions such as love and hate "bring perdurance and permanence for the first time to our existence."[54] In other words, our enduring passions are constitutive of our ongoing human existence in relation to the concretized, *a priori* structure of being-in-the-world. Contemporary emotional theories, by and large, do not discriminate between the momentary seizures of affects and the long-term passions. In contrast, Heidegger's rudimentary field theory of consciousness, in which we are moodily related to our world and to one another, enables him to elucidate that our emotional feelings, specifically our passions, "bring permanence for the first time to our existence" as human beings. As feeling beings, we know being and

---

51. Ibid., 47.
52. Tallon, *Head and Heart*, 100.
53. Heidegger, "Will as Affect, Passion, and Feeling," 48.
54. Ibid., 49.

time. Our feeling-being is the basis on which we come to know ourselves as temporal beings.[55] Understood in this way, *Angst* is a mood or long-term emotion and as such is not amenable to any analysis that is reductive of its temporal exclusivity[56] anymore than it is amenable to an analysis that is ignorant of its intentional character.

In summary to this point, "feeling" is the genus; momentary "affect" and enduring "passion" are the species. Now we are in position to appreciate what Heidegger means when he tells us that an emotional feeling is a resolute or undeniable openness of human beings to other beings: "A feeling is the way we find ourselves in relationship to beings, and thereby at the same time to ourselves. It is the way we find ourselves particularly attuned to beings which we are not and to the being we ourselves are."[57] Let us suppose that *Angst* as such is a feeling that discloses something about us as human beings in our world. Following Heidegger, let us call this something "attunement." What is it about the phenomenon of *Angst*, when we think in terms of its quasi-intentionality in the context of a field theory of consciousness, that enables us to know nature by way of our natural attunement?

In *Being and Time,* Heidegger speaks to this in technical detail, but the essentials are put more prosaically in our present text from Heidegger's "Will as Affect, Passion, and Feeling." A feeling or *Gefühl* is our irrefragable attunement to being, our own and the being of others. This is an open realism, if I may put it this way. There is nothing idealistic in this analysis of a feeling. By virtue of our kind of existence, the *Dasein* kind of existence, as we read in *Being and Time,* we are always turned on and tuned in to our human being and to the being of others, something like the all-bands receiver of a fanatic amateur radio club that is constantly on the air, at the same time broadcasting a "CQ" invitation to any other station to respond and listening as well for input signals. The ham club is thus constantly attuned. A feeling is the "felt sense" of our attunement or "mood."[58] We could say from the context of Heidegger's

---

55. For an elaboration of temporality in light of our feeling-being, see Richard Polt's analysis of Heideggerian "guilt" as owning up to our indebtedness to the past and our responsibility toward the future in Polt, *Heidegger*, 88–92.

56. Johansson, *Ontological Investigations*, 106–9.

57. Ibid., 51.

58. Gendlin, "*Befindlichkeit*," passim, esp. endnote 4.

Nietzsche lectures that emotion and mood are more specific terms for "feeling" in this respect.

A feeling is our disposition or mood toward everything or toward "what is on the whole."[59] This is its nonobjective (in the sense of its whole-world) intentionality or what I have been calling its quasi-intentionality. An affect such as anger is a quick, short-term disposition; a passion such as hate is a settled, long-term disposition. An affect is like the weather of our being whereas a passion is our climate. Without our thinking about it, a feeling or mood is the way we relate to our world, and after we have thought it through or demurred to consider it, a feeling is the way we relate to our world. A feeling is like the carrier wave being received on the ham club's receiver, with or without the CW or Morse code having yet been deciphered. There is "something there," and it is not mere static, but exactly what its content is may remain to be determined if the station operator is only automatically "hearing one and copying one" Morse code character after another, as radio operators say. He knows that there is something meaningful there, but he does not at this point pause to consider what it signifies. Or a feeling may be like the carrier wave being received by a station operator who is raptly attentive to every nuance of the "fist" of the station operator who is keying the incoming signal such that the receiving operator is at the same time in perfect tune with the message and with the means by which it is being broadcast to him. So, saying that we are attuned to our world or that we are in a mood is to say that we exist in such a way that we are disposed toward or "open to" other beings. When we are being inauthentic, then, like the Morse code copier on automatic pilot, we are still attuned but are oblivious to what is going on. Thus the feeling seems meaningless. When we are being authentic, we are both attuned and consciously aware of everything involved in the message and in the whole ongoing process. In this case, the feeling is meaningful.

An emotional feeling is an undeniable, but not always cognized, feature of our ongoing or "perduring" relation with other beings, our *Mitsein*, in a field of consciousness. A feeling is always a feeling-of-the-world, of our situation as human beings already immersed in reality. Because of our being human beings, we are feeling beings. Or we could

---

59. See Hans-Georg Gadamer's reminiscences on this phrase of Heidegger's in his "Martin Heidegger's One Path," 19–34, esp. 29.

just as well say that because we are feeling beings we are human beings capable of interpreting being, what Heidegger calls *Dasein*.

To be sure, our feelings are not the validation of our situation as a cognitive conclusion, something we arrive at after a calculation of some sort. As Wittgenstein says in *Philosophical Investigations*, the validation of a feeling "is not like calculating rules."[60] But neither is our feeling irrational in the sense of being dismissible as nonsensical or meaningless. It is our natural condition. It is our natural condition known naturally via our emotional being. In other words, our emotional feelings are known phenomenologically, and are understood existentially. The failure to attend to the phenomena as such is a cognitive failure and is not due to the nature of our feelings, but to the unnatural (or we could say "to the de-naturing") presuppositions of our theories. Such an attention deficit, once noticed, ought to lead us to search for more ontologically robust neuroscientific theories that can accommodate the phenomenon of mood.

A feeling can then be investigated, philosophically and scientifically, for what it discloses about our natural condition. If a mood is intentional, then this disclosure will tell us something significant about ourselves, perhaps, as with Heidegger, even about our responsibility as persons who are anxious about our own temporal existence in the world. This is what we mean by referring to what we can know by paying attention to our feelings as disclosive truth. Our feelings, such as everyday fear or *Angst*, disclose how it is with us for the time being. As we think about our feelings, the fact that we feel discloses what kind of being we are and, at the same time, that being is a concern for us. On this understanding, our feeling of *Angst* is an objective phenomenon meriting further scientific investigation.

Although it is commonplace to regard ourselves as thinking subjects or spectators, isolated from the world of objects and other subjects by an epistemological glass ceiling, our feelings are an indication that we are, willy-nilly, "coping beings"[61] already immersed in the world and already in relation to other beings. We do not merely perceive others; rather, we are ourselves in tune with others. Our being resonates with their being. This follows naturally from our nature, from our being hu-

---

60. Wittgenstein, *Philosophical Investigations*, 227 (German) and 227e (English).
61. Magee, *The Great Philosophers*, 258.

man beings in the natural world. And this intentionality of our feelings gives us something to think about.

In support of a fundamental criticism of the study of these feelings by means of scientific analysis—as Heidegger writes a decade earlier in *Being and Time*, *Angst*, as a component of conscience is "prior to psychological description and beyond any biological 'explanation'"[62]—Heidegger begins his subsequent Nietzsche lecture "Will as Affect, Passion, and Feeling" with a caveat regarding the submission of philosophy to science. Here is the fuller text that I have been working from:

> We cannot deny that the things physiology grapples with—particular states of the body, changes in internal secretions, muscle flexions, occurrences in the nervous system—are also proper to affects, passions, and feelings. But *we have to ask whether all these bodily states and the body itself are grasped in a metaphysically adequate way*, so that one may without further ado borrow material from physiology and biology, as Nietzsche, to his own detriment, so often did. The one fundamental point to realize here is that no result of any science can ever be applied *immediately* to philosophy.[63]

The physiological aspects ought not to be utterly denied in a comprehensive study of emotional feelings, of course. But neither ought our feelings, such as our feeling of anguish, be reduced to their physiological concomitants,[64] for scientific and philosophical reasons that I shall explain in detail in the next chapter. The physical substrates of our feelings may be taken as necessary conditions for certain aspects of our feeling nature,[65] although admittedly this is not considered in Heidegger's existential analysis of these phenomena, but the physical substrata are not our feelings per se.

In this vein, let me note that it is not just that philosophers stand in need of neuroscientific theory in order to validate the ability of moods, such as *Angst*, to reveal the human condition. It is also the case that neuroscientists stand in need of philosophers like Heidegger to critique

---

62. Heidegger, *Being and Time*, 248.

63. Heidegger, "Will as Affect, Passion, and Feeling," 45. Italics added.

64. This is another way of maintaining what Professor Tallon refers to as "the irreducible intentionality" of our affects. See Tallon, *Head and Heart*, 4, 35, 79, 123, 205.

65. See, for example, the suggestion of the role of mirror neurons in Becchio and Bertone, discussed in the third chapter of the present dissertation, "Wittgenstein Running," 123–33.

their emotional theorizing. Heidegger's criticism of Nietzsche's scientism in his Nietzsche lectures applies as well to theorists in our century who carry along the presuppositions of earlier versions of neuroscience, immediately and uncritically, into their theories of emotion.

Consider here Antonio Damasio's *Looking for Spinoza: Joy, Sorrow, and the Feeling Brain*. In earlier books this popular neuroscientist addressed the role of emotion and decision-making[66] and the role of feeling and emotion in the construction of the self,[67] but this is his most recent "progress report on the nature and *human significance* of feelings and related phenomena."[68] Damasio, undeniably sensitive to human beings as feeling persons, construes feelings essentially as somatic perceptions. "As I see it, the *origin* of the perceptions that constitute the essence of feeling is clear: There is a general object, the body, and there are many parts to that object that are continuously mapped in a number of brain structures."[69] He employs these somatic perceptions that are "continuously mapped" in, or perhaps we could say are "continuously mapped *within*," unspecified brain structures as the contents of our feelings. "The *contents* of those perceptions are also clear: varied body states portrayed by the body-representing maps along a range of possibilities."[70] Damasio thus construes the essential nature of feelings that are simultaneously perceptions of physical events and physical events themselves in biometric terms.

What might a neuroscientist such as Damasio gain from an intentional analysis of feeling such as I am arguing? Well, Damasio takes the body itself to be the formal object of emotional feelings. At the same time, he construes emotional feelings as bodily feelings themselves. He refers to the functioning of the micro- and macrostructure of muscles in the body and in the heart and tells us, "The particular states of those body components, as portrayed in the brain's body maps, is a content of the perceptions that constitute feelings."[71] His working hypothesis is that emotional feelings are feelings *about* physical feelings and that physical feelings are, at the same time, the substrata of emotional feelings.

66. Damasio, *Descartes' Error*.
67. Damasio, *The Feeling of What Happens*.
68. Damasio, *Looking for Spinoza*, 6, italics added.
69. Ibid., 87.
70. Ibid.
71. Ibid.

That is to say, one's (emotional) feelings are essentially one's (physical) feelings of one's (physical) feelings. On my intentional analysis, Damasio is engaging in circular reasoning at some level.

Perhaps it could be objected that Damasio's account is not circular, but only mildly self-referential—like a picture of a picture. An objector could plausibly point out that, as with all mental entities, feelings are brain states. Further (the objector could continue), feelings are brain states that are *about* other parts of the body that represent or carry information from other parts of the body and from within other parts of the brain itself. Thus brain states are *about* brain states. This objection does not, however, account for affective intentionality. This disclosed circularity—certainly not a vicious circularity for the neurology of brain states in general—may nevertheless indicate that emotional feelings with quasi-intentionality (that is, moods that are *about* the whole world, though in an undefined manner) cannot be completely verified scientifically in terms of the human brain considered in isolation from its external environment, but are better studied in a field of relationships, in a field of being-in-the-world. This indicates the need for, as Thomas Kuhn would say, a paradigm shift on the part of the neuroscientist, not in respect of his neurological explanations exactly, but in terms of the viability of his neurological model as it pertains to cognitive emotions. Heidegger offers such a scientific paradigm to which we may shift our thinking.

SUMMARY

In light of his field theory of consciousness as suggested by his analysis of *Angst*, we can consider in more depth how Heidegger validates a feeling according to the concept of mood or *Stimmung*. It is noteworthy for his existential analysis that "feeling" is not a noun only but a participle. We are not cogitating, Cartesian beings who happen to have feelings; rather, we are feeling beings. We can also say that we are, as feeling beings, in touch with being. For Heidegger, feeling is thus a disclosure of existence. Our "feeling being" is a disclosure of a particular kind. The contemplation of our feeling-experience discloses the phenomenon of mood or *Stimmung*. Even though as *Dasein* we human beings can normally dominate whatever mood we are in with knowledge and will, that is, we can affect the weather and even, over time, the climate of our being, nevertheless the first fact is that "mood is a primordial kind of being for Da-sein in which it is disclosed to itself *before* all cognition and willing and *beyond* their scope of disclosure."[72] That we have a mood, that we are never mood-less, is the insight here. This is an ontological characteristic of our attunement or *Befindlichkeit*: "The *first* essential ontological characteristic of attunement is: *Attunement discloses Da-sein in its thrownness* . . ."[73] In other words, attunement indicates, as I have been arguing, at least an implicit field theory of consciousness as it brings to light the intentionality of our feelings and the wider undefined natural horizon within which we find ourselves as beings tuned to other beings. Here we all are, situated in, and naturally attuned to one another within our ontological habitat.

In order to maintain our attention to *Angst* in the field, so to speak, we will want to bear in mind that a feeling or mood is a primordial, a pre-theoretical, an existentially "'bare' way of being for man. Our 'mood' is constitutive of our selves and our world, it structures them. Mood discloses 'state of mind' (*Befindlichkeit*) as the way we are as *In-der-Welt-seins* (being-in-the-world)."[74] Although our thinking and willing can lead us variously to interpret, to misinterpret, and to want to alter or to maintain our present mood, still we ought to note well that we are always in one mood or another. We humans are always feeling beings. We are always *In-der-Welt-sein*. Knowing this, we are aware of a world in which we subsist in a feeling and human manner.

But our feelings, I must reiterate, most especially our feeling of *Angst*, are not themselves the result or product of our thinking and willing. Our feelings or moods are the first datum, if you will, upon which our thinking and willing go to work. As a feeling or mood, *Angst* is what it is apart from our cognition and our volition. "Mood assails. It comes neither from 'without' nor from 'within,' but rises from being-in-the-world itself as a mode of that being."[75] In this way, the impulse to validate a feeling by establishing its cognitive pedigree is rendered moot. A feeling can be assessed in the manner Searle recommends, namely, as a mental state legitimized by its directedness toward some external and therefore more objective state of affairs. But the manner of assessment does not make a feeling or affection, or more specifically, an emotion or

72. Ibid., 128.
73. Ibid.
74. Del Nevo, "What Exactly Is Feeling Then, According to Heidegger?," 1.
75. Heidegger, *Being and Time*, 129.

a mood, what it is. A mood is our appraisal of the entire state of affairs; it is not a cognition of specific extramental objects or classes of objects, defined in one way or another.

This is not a metaphorical or folk psychology account; this is indeed the constitution and function of our feelings. Before we know, we feel. Before we want to achieve knowledge, we feel. Our being as feeling beings thus makes us part and parcel of the natural world already, even before we come to give it a second thought, or indeed before we give it a first thought. This is uniquely the case in regard to our feeling of *Angst*. "Da-sein is anxious in the very ground of its being"[76] whether she contemplates or ignores this anxiousness.

On the understanding that the technical elements of mood and attunement in *Being and Time* can be more prosaically defined as "feeling" in the context of Heidegger's later "What Is Metaphysics?" and Nietzsche lectures, we can now summarize and paraphrase Heidegger on intentionality and our feeling of anguish this way: Although it is true that by thinking about our feeling of *Angst* and determining to do something about it we can alter our mood, it remains the case that before we start thinking about it and before we can will it to be otherwise, we are, in a meaningful manner, *assailed* by our feeling of *Angst*. Apart from our cognition and our volition, our feeling nature shows us that we are, contra Descartes, already engaged with the world on the whole. We always are. Thus, feeling *Angst* is not merely an interior psychological event, nor is it some sort of mysterious conduit by which we might emerge from our inner mental life into the outer world! This sense of outreach is a secondary characteristic of our feeling. Rather, our feeling *Angst* is fundamental and basic. Such a feeling is, by virtue of its intentionality, an irrefragable link with our as-yet-undefined world. It opens up the horizon or ground on which our objective knowledge goes to work. Objective intentionality follows upon, and does not itself ground, the horizons at which our moods aim. Only as the kind of being that feels can life matter to us at all. The fact that things matter to us is a consequence of our existence as feeling beings. So, you see, our feelings are the basis for our thoughts and decisions about ourselves and for our ongoing engagement with the world.[77]

76. Ibid., 177.
77. Compare ibid., 128–29.

Heidegger's claim needs to be validated empirically, which is the task of my third chapter. In this first chapter I have simply asked Heidegger to set the scene and state the terms of the discussion. Indeed, he may even be said to anticipate the method needed to validate and thus support his claim that moods are intentional, namely, by finding a way of getting past Cartesian materialism and finding human being first and foremost, always and already, in-the-world. In the next chapter, I explain how earlier generations of neuroscientific theories, by presupposing a form of Cartesian materialism, are inadequate to the task of validating the feeling of *Angst*.

TWO

Toward an Affective Neuroscience of Mood

[E]xtroversion is a basic characteristic of the biological pattern of experience. The bodily basis of the senses in the sense organs, the functional correlation of sensations with the positions and movements of the organs, the imaginative, conative, emotive consequences of sensible presentations, and the resulting local movements of the body, all indicate that elementary experience is concerned, not with the immanent aspects of living, but with its external conditions and opportunities. Within the full pattern of living, there is a partial, intermittent, extroverted pattern of conscious living.

—Bernard Lonergan, "The Biological Pattern of Existence"
in *Insight*[1]

WE NEED A SECOND chapter on Heidegger to offer what can be interpreted as his manner of showing how a claim to the validity of *Angst* can be supported, namely, by moving the site of the explanation from inside *Dasein* into the world in which *Dasein* exists. This entails an adumbration of an affective neuroscience that will resist the reduction of the subjective phenomenon of moods to the neurological affect systems of basic emotions. Please note that my intentionality thesis that a mood such as *Angst* is objectively verified in terms of its intentionality toward the world as a whole does not contradict current affective neuroscience. My thesis nevertheless calls for a fuller, more robust account of intentionality than is currently available in cognitive neuroscience, for example, in the writings of Searle and Griffiths, among others.

1. Longernan, *Insight*, 108.

INTRODUCTION

One current trend in philosophy of mind is to describe *Angst* or anxiety as nothing more than a specific activity of an individual organism's neurology, much as fear is nothing more than the activity of an affect program. On the one hand, this trend fails to differentiate between basic emotions, higher cognitive emotions, and the moods based on them. In the present thesis, basic emotions such as fear are understood as lower emotions that can be essentially and operationally defined according to their respective affect programs. Basic emotions are relatively autonomic and brief. Higher emotions entail a certain amount of cognition over time. Moods such as *Angst* are, according to my thesis, long-term higher emotions that endure over time to such an extent that our cognitive and emotional being, perhaps even features of the architecture of our brains, is shaped by the manner in which they dispose us toward the entire natural world.

On the other hand, this trend to reduce anxiety to its biology, as if *Angst* were nothing more than its biological substrate, follows a popular notion that brain states admit of explanations that begin and end within the brain itself. In what I shall refer to as "previous-generation neuroscience," the famous Cartesian bridge between a spiritual (unextended) mind and a material (extended) body had been translated into a bridge between a material brain housing the self and a material body as the instrument by which the self, reducible for all intents and purposes to a self-contained brain, may reach out to its environment, with more or less success. This is a position that Rockwell calls "Cartesian materialism." In the wake of Descartes, it was commonly accepted that the *full* explanation of consciousness lay in the brain, and only in the brain, of a conscious organism. Rockwell argues for the need to include other brains as well in our account of aspects of human consciousness. If he is correct (and I am arguing that he is), then we have to seek an account of *Angst* in the social dimension. It is in this *social* dimension that we find sufficient context to account for intentionality. There is, interestingly, a neuroscientific push toward the social dimension, in the case of neuroscience and moods. This impulse comes from the inability of affective neuroscience to identify a "mood system" analogous to the affect systems of basic emotions.

What is of interest for my thesis as to how anxiety is verifiable as a mood is this additional fact that has recently come to light in the science of affective neuroscience, namely, that experts in affective neuroscience acknowledge a substantial difficulty in accounting for anxiety in terms of brain systems, in such a self-contained, systemic manner as ought to be possible if, that is, Cartesian materialism were the case. For example, Jaak Panksepp observes that since 1979, a number of brain systems have been proposed as anxiety systems. Each of these theories remains controversial, especially as animals that have had these proposed anxiety systems experimentally damaged continue to exhibit anxious behavior.[2] The clinical data are what led Panksepp to explain that from a neuroscientific viewpoint the simplification of the pertinent issues—what I have been analyzing as a reduction of *Angst* to the cognitive, or to what Griffiths calls the natural categories of biology—may be hampering our scientific study of affects such as anxiety. And so, I would like to ask at this point, why not extend the field of consciousness from within the brain of a solitary individual to the social, intersubjective field?

My proposal is that we begin to consider whether the current state of contradictory clinical data might indicate that we cannot achieve a definitive understanding of anxiety by looking solely *within* the (solitary) mammalian brain, but could do better by expanding the field of investigation to the world in which that brain exists and toward which its emotional systems are intentionally structured. Perhaps the clinical data open the door on a wider, nonreductive neuroscience of anxiety. A reductive understanding of *Angst* is one that seeks to understand the complex phenomenon of this mood in terms of the properties or functions of its elements, or of one set of its constituent elements. Speaking more formally, reductionism is the claim that that the elements of the whole (in this case, of the conscious experience of *Angst*) are ontologically prior to the experience as we have it. In addition, there is a presumed chain of causation that runs predominately from the elements to the whole.[3]

As to my resistance to reductive theories of moods, I have in mind the irreducibility of consciousness put forth a few years ago by John Searle, which I take to be of particular importance for neuroscientific discussions of emotions and moods.[4] Searle's concern is that the effort

---

2. See Panksepp, *Affective Neuroscience*, 212–13.

3. A source for my understanding of reductionism is Rose, Lewontin, and Kamin, *Biology, Ideology and Human Nature*.

4. Searle, *Mind, Language, and Society*, 55–62.

to report on subjective phenomena with scientific objectivity effectively strips the subjective phenomenon under study of its subjective character. It is his contention that "the subjectivity of consciousness makes it irreducible to third-person phenomena, according to the standard models of scientific reduction."[5] This is so because consciousness is unlike digestion. As Searle explains, once we have achieved a scientific description of the micro-processes of enzymes and renin in the breakdown of carbohydrates, this is the whole account of the phenomenon of digestion. However, once we have achieved a scientific explanation of the micro-processes of neurons and neurological systems—although please note that there is no such system available to us to account for anxiety—or even an explanation of quantum-processes, we do not have a whole account of *Angst*. We still have phenomenon left over. As I shall discuss in the next chapter, Searle's notion of moods is itself reductionist, and so, while I am adopting his theoretical caution for my own argument, I do not accept his theory of moods.

Drawing on Searle's caution against such scientific "nothing-but" theories ("A mood is *nothing but* a complex of affect systems"), it seems clear that there can be a number of types of scientific reductions, including *eliminative* reductions and *noneliminative* reductions.[6] An eliminative reduction would treat a mood as an illusion, theoretically eliminating the *felt* phenomenon as a phenomenon. A noneliminative reduction would reduce the phenomenon to what we used to call its "atomic" reality or, as we say at present, to its quantum reality. Neither reduction is suitable for properties of consciousness inasmuch as we would then be excising subjectivity from our study of this aspect of consciousness. Nonetheless, consciousness, including as it does the phenomena of higher emotions and moods, "has a first-person ontology, and we cannot for that reason perform a reduction on consciousness that we can on third-person phenomena..."[7] Taking Searle's point for now, I would also say that I do not acknowledge that emotions and moods are constrained to first-person ontologies only. I take it that "first-person ontology" was a valid way of describing our experience of mood phenomenologically, whereas a third-person ontology, a scientific account, is clearly required for emotional theorizing today.

5. Ibid., 55.
6. See ibid., 55–57.
7. Ibid., 57.

Now the undue simplifying or reduction of *Angst* on the assumption of "Cartesian materialism" was, as I have suggested, already envisioned by Heidegger in his well-known idea that *Dasein* is *In-der-Welt-Sein*. Merleau-Ponty's thesis of the body's intentionality[8] is evidence that Heidegger anticipated social analyses of human existence, as is Emmanuel Levinas's thesis of the primacy of the ethical,[9] both of which proceed on the basis of Heidegger's version of affective intentionality. Heidegger analyzes the mind (if I may put it this way) as being-in-the-world. In a similar vein, Teed Rockwell[10] argues the obsolescence of scientific models of mind-as-brain or mind-as-brain-plus-body, and argues instead for a paradigm of mind as brain-body-world. Thus an emerging, next-generation neuroscience supports my thesis that moods such as *Angst* require a suitable field theory for scientific analysis. In this emerging neuroscience, biology, although it is the basis and the beginning of the study of moods, is not the end of the story.

To indicate why and how this is so, we shall consider the necessity as well as the insufficiency of biological substrates to account for *Angst* inasmuch as *Angst* is categorically unlike the process of digestion (a mood has a first-person ontology; digestion does not) and furthermore is unlike a basic emotion such as fear (fear is explainable on the basis of its affect system, with no phenomenon left over).

As a case in point, Paul Griffiths has been contending that moods ought to be construed in terms of "biological homologies," on his reductive understanding of mood as a matter of affect programs *simpliciter*. Griffiths, of course, is aware of the conceptual difficulties of equating moods and basic emotions. As a psychologist, he is aware in addition of the contradictory clinical data behind recent efforts to identify anxiety systems within the brain. Therefore, he is careful to avoid further

---

8. See, for example, Merleau-Ponty, "An Unpublished Text by Merleau-Ponty," 3–11. Commenting on his *Phenomenology of Perception,* Merleau-Ponty writes, "Our body is not in space like things. . . . For us the body is much more than an instrument or a means; it is our expression in the world, the visible form of our intentions. Even our most secret affective movements, those most deeply tied to the humoral infrastructure, help to shape our perception of things."

9. See, for example, Levinas, *Ethics and Infinity,* 39–41: "In *Sein und Zeit*'s analyses of anxiety, care and being-toward-death we witness a sovereign exercise of phenomenology . . . existence itself, as through the affect of an intentionality, is animated by a meaning . . ."

10. Rockwell, *Neither Brain Nor Ghost.*

scientific elaborations of this reduction of moods for the most part. All the same, he fails, when addressing *moods*, to verify them in terms of affect programs with anything like the success he has in analyzing basic emotions in terms of affect programs. In my view, he opens a door into a neuroscientific study of moods without actually stepping through.

I would like us to take a few steps into the wider neuroscience suggested but not developed by neurotheorists such as Griffiths. I do not, of course, deny the necessity of biological substrates for our mood of *Angst*. It seems beyond debate that, given the effectiveness of Prozac and other pharmacological regimens, there is a biological aspect to our moods. My question continues to be whether the biology is a sufficient condition to account for the human experience of *Angst*. In the wake of the insufficiency of any homologous theory of emotion to account for our moods in terms merely of shared internal physical structures, I am simply unpacking Heidegger in order to argue, not for another sort of dualism, but for the scientific viability of an emergentist, weak supervenience theory of mind that is attentive to this mood's intentionality.

This theory is "weak" insofar as the brain and its neurophysiological processes are regarded as necessary but not sufficient conditions to explain higher emotions and moods such as *Angst* as "engagements with the world."[11] Further, as this necessitates the consideration of intentionality, a category not on the radar screen of emotional theorists who address the phenomenon of moods solely from the standpoint of affective programs, I am offering this as a philosophical contribution to the neuroscientific investigation of moods inasmuch as the intentional property of *Angst*, in this instance, calls for an upgrade in the *kind* of neuroscience required to study this mood. The "emergentist" aspect of my view depends upon the neuroscientific understanding that "mind" (I am reverting for the moment to the more familiar locution of mind-as-brain) is both *hierarchical*—the higher or cortical builds on the lower or subcortical—and it is *modular* in that the affective and cognitive do not reduce to one another. This is due, according to Panksepp, to different evolutionary developments, different locations, and different chemistries. The emergentist aspect is a property dualism but does not entail an ontological dualism. That is to say, the difficulty here is conceptual

---

11. See Solomon, "Emotions as Engagements with the World." Solomon seems to regard emotions as a kind of thinking, whereas my thesis is that the mood of *Angst* is a different kind of intentionality. Mood is not reducible to cognition or volition.

or paradigmatic. Rather than failing to consider the intentionality of a mood—rather than promoting a reductive model of a mood in order to make all moods fit within our paradigm of basic emotions on the supposition that moods must be construed as nothing more than another type of affect system—why not contemplate scientifically how a higher dimension of explanation is required to explain our higher emotions? Further, let us note that basic emotions and higher-order moods such as *Angst* are alike in that they are intentional.

AFFECTIVE NEUROSCIENCE-PLUS

In a recent book from Oxford Press, William Irvine argues that our basic, animal emotions account for our feelings of anxiety: "I would argue, by the way, that the emotions are the source of these anxieties. Besides tempting us with possibilities for pleasure . . . the emotions are capable of apprehensive whispers . . ."[12] There is nothing philosophically remarkable in this assumption that anxiety is of a kind with our basic emotions. But is this customary, unremarkable analysis of our emotions and of our feeling *Angst* scientifically adequate? The question we may then ask is whether the same neuroscientific analysis, widely accepted for scientific studies of the so-called "basic emotions," is adequate for the phenomenon of *Angst*.

This presents us with a question of space as well as a question of time. Moods are commonly defined in contrast with emotions at least by their longer duration. Sometimes they are defined vis-à-vis emotions by their lower intensity (although some moods are so intense as to lead individuals to suicide). Sometimes moods are "spatially" relegated more to the background than the foreground of our consciousness.

To begin this neuroscientific evaluation of moods, let me reiterate the caveat from Heidegger. Speaking of his nonordinary analysis of conscience, he cautions us against reductive accounts of our actual human experiences: "The ontological analysis of conscience . . . is prior to any psychological description and classification of experiences of conscience, just as it lies outside any biological 'explanation,' that is, dissolution of this phenomenon."[13] As I have already mentioned in my discussion of an implicit, abbreviated field theory apparent in *Being and Time* and in his

---

12. Irvine, *On Desire*, 82.
13. Heidegger, *Being and Time*, 248.

Nietzsche lectures, Heidegger does not deny altogether the necessity of physiological states for emotional analysis. It is just that he does not consider their physiology to be the whole story. Intellectual honesty leads me to say as well that I do not read Heidegger as being concerned with scientific validation or, more precisely, with neuroscientific verification of any sort for his philosophy. This lack of concern with scientific verification is something that twenty-first century phenomenologists would not find acceptable. This is why my project of *validating* a feeling such as *Angst* entails scientific *verification*.

Validation is a way of securing the cognitive and human worth of emotions and moods by conceptual analysis. This is usually the goal of theorists of emotion who espouse what Leslie Brothers calls "the *language of the mind*."[14] My thesis is based in part on the conviction that a twenty-first century validation of a mood also ought to entail scientific *verification*. Verification is way of investigating the nature of emotions and moods by scientific methodologies. This is usually associated with theorists of emotion who espouse what Brothers calls "the *language of science*."[15] My thesis proceeds as well from the conviction that current methods for verifying basic emotions are insufficient for verifying *moods*. For this reason, a neuroscience of moods can benefit from the conceptual insights of philosophers who pursue theories of emotions and moods in the language of the mind. In short, we need a "language of moods."

Noting Heidegger's last-generation phenomenology-without-science, if the phenomenon of conscience lies beyond biological explanation and precedes psychological description, the same can be said of "the fundamental attunement of *Angst*"[16] which is for Heidegger the linchpin of his existential analysis of conscience. Are we then obliged to leave *Angst* in the past as a relic of early twentieth-century existentialism? Not if a scientific *verification* of this mood is possible. As I have indicated, this is not a dissertation on Heidegger per se, but a project that welcomes Heidegger's insight that moods have intentionality. His discovery seems today to call for neuroscientific verification. And so, I am not at all following Heidegger in eschewing altogether a scientific verification of a mood such as *Angst*. I am, however, following him in questioning the

14. Brothers, *Friday's Footprint*, 142.
15. Ibid.
16. Heidegger, *Being and Time*, 255.

sufficiency of our mapping of interior neurological processes as the be-all and end-all of a suitable study of moods.

In the current literature, *Angst* is almost always treated as a species of emotion that is, in turn, considered almost exclusively within the structure of the individual organism's brain. Following Heidegger's insight, I would say that we do better to construe emotions as short-term indicators of our existence as mood-oriented beings in a field of consciousness expansive enough to embrace our neurology *plus* the world on the whole. So, before we can thoughtfully consider the primordial role of a mood such as *Angst* for our human being, we require a suitably robust affective neuroscience in which moods can be studied as moods and not be reduced a priori to more scientifically familiar categories. That is, we need to reconsider the type of neuroscientific view that sees moods and emotions alike as nothing more than internal biological phenomena, explicable predominately in terms of elements within the skin of the individual. In order to illustrate what I have in mind regarding the next logical step for us to take in respect to the neuroscientific task of studying and validating the phenomenon of *Angst*, I shall first take a step back and turn to the work of the neuropsychologist Paul Griffiths.

To his 1997 book, *What Emotions Really Are*, Griffiths appends a concluding chapter titled "Coda—Mood and Emotion." He concludes that it is plausible to suggest "that moods are neurochemical states, which act to modify the activities of broad areas of the central nervous system."[17] While maintaining that "mood phenomena correspond to genuine explanatory kinds at two levels," namely, what he identifies as "the computational level" and "the implementation level," Griffiths argues for an explanation of mood that is heavily weighted toward internal, biological processes, so much so that the internal biological structure of the individual organism is taken to be the container of emotion. That is, he recommends the study of moods within the purview of his theory of basic emotions. In subsequent elaborations to this depiction of what emotions and moods "really are," Griffiths elaborates his reductive view.

At the same time, there are (in terms of my present thesis) intriguing suggestions of a higher dimension of scientific investigation. For example, the biological homologues that he makes the basis for any and all genuinely scientific studies of emotion and emotions (including moods) are homologous with—what, exactly?—neurophysiological

---

17. Griffiths, *What Emotions Really Are*, 255.

"hardware," or "wetware," or with other, similarly-structured individuals? Doesn't Griffiths' analysis of homological similarity depend, in turn, on shared activity within a social field? It seems to me that Griffiths may have in mind as his theoretical model of emotion an anatomical model of the brain ("*This* region is the site of the affect program for fear, so *where* is anxiety located?"). Griffiths seems overall determined to carry on his work within the individual brain, but his presuppositions appear to include a social field, what I have called an "inter-cranial" world of others who matter to the individual in a way that goes beyond cognitive assessments of truth, interest, and information.

This, I think, is the uniqueness or irreducibility of our higher-emotional and moodful intentionality: in a mood such as *Angst*, we intend the world as value, worth, and importance, whereas in cognition, we intend the world as truth and information. The problem with Griffiths's reductive analysis of mood is not his attention to the neurological substrates of our emotions and moods, but his tendency toward noneliminative reduction, toward an emotional theory that, in the case of moods, leaves us with more phenomenon still to account for. This conflation of a mood such as anxiety with basic emotions such as fear has consequences for research. One consequence is the predilection for studying the phenomenon of *Angst* exclusively in terms of what is going on inside an individual's brain.

It is interesting for the present study that Heidegger too contemplates the phenomenon of fear in order to make a painstaking differentiation between his analysis of fear, an emotion, and his analysis of *Angst*, a mood. Griffiths seems inclined, on the basis of his type of neuroscientific explanation, to maintain that mood ought to be studied *under* the category of fear, a basic emotion, on a broadly functionalist understanding.[18] What I am saying here is that Griffiths's neuroscientific recognition that an organism's basic emotions, though predominately a matter of internal processes, situate the organism within a world to which it reacts and adapts is scientifically valuable, as far as it goes. But it does not go far enough into the Heidegger territory, so to speak. Notwithstanding the value of his conclusions regarding basic emotions, as we progress to the

---

18. See Kim, *Mind in a Physical World*, 101: "[T]he functionalist conception of mental properties is *required* for mind-body reduction. In fact it is necessary and sufficient for reducibility. If this is right, mind-body reductionism and the functionalist approach to mentality stand or fall together; they share the same metaphysical fate."

higher emotions, the external moorings, if you will, the intentional interaction of the organism with a wider and wider world becomes more critical for a thorough (scientific and phenomenological) account of the phenomenon. Recall as well Panksepp's conclusion that the clinical data regarding anxiety are not only inconclusive as to which brain systems are its substrate, but that the clinical data for proposed systemic substrates to this mood are in fact contradictory.

In the case of his preliminary explanation of a mood, Griffiths's functionalist construal fails to address what I have been referring to as a mood's quasi-intentionality. This is presumably because the intentional ties that bind the mood to what it is *about*—and please recall that the formal object of mood is not a specific perceived threat or a proximate innerworldly object, but the undefined world as a whole—do not necessarily contribute to the survival performances (that is, to the functions, broadly understood) of the "human organism" and therefore tend to be excised in Griffiths' functional analysis. This attentiveness only to the organism's function within its proximate environment contravenes my working hypothesis that the intentionality of the mood moors the human being to the world as a whole and thus grounds not utilitarian outcomes but one's *conscious* situatedness.

My hypothesis began, you will recall, with Heidegger's insistence on the role of *Angst* for the recognition of *Dasein*'s individual capacity to be responsible. Now, perhaps Griffiths's explanation to date could be taken, not as an exclusion of the wider world of a mood's intentionality (*sensu negante*), but inclusively (*sensu aiente*). By this I mean to pick up the thread of intentionality that is, according to his neuroscientific analysis, a (very minor) feature of basic emotions. I will simply point out that the intentional field becomes wider as we proceed from a study of basic emotions to the higher cognitive emotions and, ultimately, to moods. Whenever Griffiths is led to contemplate moods under the category of basic emotions, he significantly restricts the field of scientific investigation, and this is the point in his diagnosis against which I am arguing for a more nuanced understanding of *Angst* in view of its higher-order, intentional character. Yet, as I have suggested, Griffiths's analysis may be taken as leaving the door open for a study of moods and their long-lasting, broad field intentionality.

If we are willing at this juncture to reconsider current neurological theory in regard to emotion, specifically in order to overcome its reductive tendency, and thus its general neglect of a social field theory, we can, I think, begin to see one reason why biological explanations of emotion and emotions, offered on the basis of brain-as-mind descriptions of fear, fail to live up to our expectations. Perhaps this will go a long way toward explaining how last-generation neuroscience might have contributed to a dismissal of our feeling of *Angst,* thereby hindering the human being's cognizance of herself in the world, or of what Heidegger would call "the authentic *Dasein.*" Perhaps a suitable type of neuroscientific study of *Angst* will go a long way toward reintroducing into the great conversation the unique potential and individual responsibility of the human being.

Reductionism, whether eliminative or noneliminative, tends to lead us not only to identify our mental states such as our emotions with brain states,[19] but to also lose the subject herself in the course of analyzing her consciousness. This entails, as I have said, the categorical error of treating an experience with a first-person ontology as if it were nothing but a nonhuman third-person object or event. This amounts to the assumption of a type-type identity, in which the experience of *Angst* is *identified with*, and thus reduced to, neural happenings entirely or mostly within the space of affect systems. Here we may give attention to the negative sense of biology-only theories of moods and higher emotions.

In respect to what is happening within the skull of the subject, the correlation between neural event and the mental property is fairly straightforward. Logically speaking, this amounts to the biconditional claim M <=> P where M is a mental event and P is a physical, that is a neurobiological, property. Ontologically speaking, if a mental event is what it is if and only if there is a specifiable neurobiological property, and if the specifiable neurological property completely accounts for the mental event, then this is, at bottom, a claim of ontological identity, M = P. Beyond this identification of neurology with emotional feeling, the M = P claim obviates any further need for the field theory of consciousness for which I have been arguing in the case of moods. *If, that is, we assume that* Angst *is essentially a mental event. But this is the very presupposition that I do not grant. My intentionality thesis argues that* Angst *is more than a mental event.* First, in respect to its intentionality

---

19. Popkin, *The Columbia History of Western Philosophy*, 658. See 633–58 for definitions of "the identity theory" and "eliminative materialism" that are utilized in this chapter.

Angst exhibits an extra-cranial property. Second, in respect to its long-term duration *Angst* is better construed as an ongoing state of mind or a temporal vector than as a momentary event.

Its extra-cranial extension (the major dimension of my analysis) and its long-term or "perduring" character as well make the human experience of this mood unlike the basic emotions in respect to its being in time. The identification of neurological properties with the emotions themselves makes scientific sense in the case of basic emotions that are held in common by both humans and nonhuman animals. Basic emotions are localized within their affect systems and are of relatively brief duration. It does not seem remiss to portray such basic emotions as fear or anger in ways that assume a kind of stimulus-response relationship with a person's or animal's relationship to the environment. The presence of a threat causes a similar fear response in a tomcat as in a poet laureate.

Briefly noted, the category of basic emotion is not a settled issue among emotional theorists generally. Craig DeLancey observes that, although a working list of basic emotions may include (but ought not be limited to): "fear, anguish, joy, sadness, disgust, seeking/curiosity, social distress, lust, care, and play," he considers fear and anger to be the subset of this list that is suitable for neuroscientific study.[20] It is worth noting in passing that DeLancey leaves anguish outside the categories of scientific inquiry. My present concern is, nevertheless, to argue that anguish or *Angst* is suitable for objective, scientific investigation in terms of its non-object or world-on-the-whole intentionality. It is critical, however, that such a scientific study takes place within a suitably large space and over a suitably lengthy time. Let me, then, return us to a sketch of the steps needed for this research into our moods.

To clarify my project as being concerned with verification in scientific terms, let me stipulate Panksepp's extensional definition in regard to DeLancey's basic emotions of fear and anger.[21] There is reason to question the sufficiency of affective neuroscience conducted within its current theoretical model as represented by the authors just mentioned for the study of anguish, as Panksepp suggests in his commentary regarding the current state of affective neuroscience in the study of anxiety. As a mood, *Angst* is better construed as a higher-level cognitive affect,

20. DeLancey, *Passionate Engines*, 28.
21. See Panksepp, *Affective Neuroscience*, 9–23, 24–40.

involving more than autonomic processes and automatic interaction with the organism's environment. *Angst* is furthermore not identifiable with any specific anxiety system within the brain. This makes anxiety *neurologically unlike* the basic emotions.

Moods can be seen as higher-level appraisals or cognition-related affects in the sense that they entail, above and beyond the homologous physiology and behaviors common both to other animals and to human beings—after all, dogs or primates have fear responses—a propositional attitude, as some philosophers of mind have said.[22] Instead of referring to "a propositional attitude," I have been speaking of our (uniquely human) conscious experience. Accordingly, in line with my stipulation of current affective neuroscience relative to *basic* emotions, I do not at all mean to downplay the neurological aspects of emotional feelings for the study of moods; only to recommend that we begin to acknowledge in our analyses that the higher the emotion, the more critical for its analysis is the need to account for the feeling's first-person ontology in respect to its spatiotemporal dimensions. I will also add that more critical is the ability to bring to the foreground the formal objects of our intentionality: the horizons, the grounds, the background by virtue of which we can investigate the intentionality of that higher-level emotion. In the established neuroscience of basic emotions, the immediate objects of our feelings of fear and anger are acknowledged components of these affects.[23] But in the category of higher emotions and moods, why must we confine ourselves to immediate intentional objects without consideration of the nonobjective world as a whole, within which the concretum or immediate object of a basic emotion comes to our attention?

The difficulty, on my intentional analysis of this mood, is that we have not yet achieved a genuine scientific investigation into *Angst* by largely confining our science to what is happening within the cranium or within the skin of a Cartesian subject, as this fails to consider this feeling within an objective structure or field of consciousness that is adequate to the investigation of the phenomenon.[24] We need at least the correctives recommended by Brothers and Rockwell, as we shall see.

---

22. For an explanation of the affective components of homology and propositional attitudes see DeLancey, *Passionate Engines*, 94–95.

23. For a discussion of concretum, the immediate objects of these basic emotions, see ibid., 89–93 and 95–97.

24. For a physicalist consideration of this point, see Kim, *Mind in a Physical World*, 57–87.

As a case in point, Griffiths maintains that a suitably scientific explanation of emotion must be a predominately neurobiological explanation. His expressed concern is that, given the present state of emotional theorizing, "emotions are not [being studied as] natural kinds." This, Griffith feels, is because emotions have not been properly explicated in terms of biology and neuroscience. In keeping with his subtitle, *The Problem of Psychological Categories*, Griffiths argues "that it is unlikely that all the psychological states and processes that fall under the vernacular category of emotion are sufficiently similar to one another to allow a unified scientific psychology of emotions"[25] To this concern Griffiths appends his conviction that such a scientific categorizing of emotion, though not realized at present, is nevertheless *the* proper goal for emotional theory.

As part and parcel of his contention that we have as yet been unable to study emotion properly, namely under the aegis of accepted neuroscientific categories as affect systems, Griffiths asserts that "evolution leads to the existence of two fundamental sets of biological categories—homologies and analogies."[26] A homologue is the same organ or physical system found in all animals and performing the same function in each individual. Analogues, on the other hand, are cases in which unrelated organs or physical systems serve a common function. A homologue is taken to indicate descent from a common ancestral form; analogues are serendipitous adaptations that allow individuals of different species to perform the same "ecological role." Categories that we might adduce analogically, Griffiths tells us, "although they might enter into useful ecological generalizations, would be systematically unsuited to the distinctive purposes of psychology and neuroscience."[27]

Here, then, is the logical epicenter of his noneliminative reduction of emotion *and moods alike*: similarities due to analogy or shared function are "shallow," whereas similarities due to homology or shared ancestry "are 'deep.'" It is this categorical constraint on the part of Griffiths that leads me to conclude that his approach is according to a negative sense. Only by interpreting him in an inclusive sense—and I admit that this may go against the grain of the body of his work thus far—can we open him up, if you will, to recognize the implicit transcendence of an

---

25. Griffiths, "Emotions as Natural Kinds," 233.
26. Ibid., 237.
27. Ibid.

intra-cranial explanation that I am recommending as the next chapter in the neuroscientific understanding of brain and world.

His methodological commitment to the explanatory value of homologies appears to work quite well for neuroscientific analyses of basic emotions such as fear for which the intentional objects are immediate and comprehensible without apparent need for the articulating of propositional attitudes and so on.[28] But is it apropos to consider *Angst* under the category of homolog? Here he runs into an insurmountable difficulty by virtue of his nothing-but theory, namely, that mood and basic emotions alike are essentially biological. One could make the case that Griffiths terminated his consideration of mood because a mood, it turns out, is not amenable to straightforward homologous analysis. For example, recall his "coda" on moods to his 1997 investigation as to what emotions really are, namely, "that moods are neurochemical states, which act to modify the activities of broad areas of the central nervous system."[29] To my knowledge, this chapter is his only sustained effort to analyze moods and is conducted on the assumption that moods are essentially complexes of basic emotions. Rather than pursuing a study of moods in terms of their quasi-intentionality or in terms of social constructivism—approaches that would in effect widen the spatiotemporal field and allow for a neuroscience of mind as brain-body-world—Griffiths remains within the cranial space of the individual (animal or human) organism even when he is seeking concourse with the wider arena of scientific emotional theorizing.

However, in his recent "Basic Emotions, Complex Emotions, Machiavellian Emotions" he concludes, "A Machiavellian perspective on the basic emotions would allow a much tighter integration of biological and cultural theories of emotion."[30] This later position seems to open up the possibility of a bridge linking biology and culture, a concourse between affective and social neuroscience. It suggests a world involvement at least for the meanings of complex and "Machiavellian" emotions. What do I mean by "world involvement"? I am thinking here of

28. See also DeLancey, *Passionate Engines*: "Finally, our growing understanding of some of the neural circuitry enabling some emotions and other affects often includes the identification of crucial roles for subcortical structures that are widely shared across mammals, and some of which may have homologs in more distantly related species," 41.

29. Griffiths, *What Emotions Really Are*, 255.

30. Griffiths, "Basic Emotions, Complex Emotions, Machiavellian Emotions," 52.

the social field, inclusive of our neurologies and those of other beings, as well as the space between—a preferable choice as the supervenience base from which our higher order emotions and moods (which Griffiths refers to as "complex emotions") emerge. And so, my question remains whether we can reduce the phenomenon of a mood to "nothing but" biology.

If Griffiths's proposed bridge between biological and cultural theories of emotion has theoretical worth, then the cultural theories of emotion ought not, on pain of equivocation, be reduced to the biological. Instead, we will need to find a means of theoretical integration. To put this another way, we will need to take care that we do not identify the cultural with the biological and thus conflate the two aspects of a mood such as *Angst*. Such conflation is somewhat benign in the case of basic emotions, but has deleterious affects on the study of higher emotions and moods. An M = P identity in the case of the basic emotions provides a fairly comprehensive understanding of what fear, for example, is all about. However, this identity becomes less and less satisfactory the higher we go (as an evolutionary psychologist or as an ontologist would say) up the ladder of rational capacities and performances. This is what generates the need for an "affective neuroscience-plus," if you will.

BEYOND BASIC EMOTIONS AND ANXIETY SYSTEMS

Let us see whether we can expand on this point with a Wittgensteinian thought experiment recommended in a standard philosophy of mind resource: "What would it be like for a researcher to *identify* someone's felt experience with a given neural process?"[31] By way of a critique of the presumed (neurological *and conscious*) similarity between our experience(s) of basic emotions, other emotions, and moods, consider an oft-cited but little-used passage from *Philosophical Investigations* regarding mental processes:

> How does the philosophical problem about mental processes and states and about behaviorism arise?—The first step is the one that altogether escapes notice. We talk of processes and states and leave their nature undecided! Sometime perhaps we shall know more about them—we think. But that is just what commits us to a particular way of looking at the matter. For we have a definite concept of what it means to learn to know a process better.

---

31. Popkin, *The Columbia History of Western Philosophy*, 659. Italics added.

(The decisive movement in the conjuring trick has been made, and it is the very one that was thought quite innocent.)—And now the analogy which was to make us understand our thoughts falls to pieces. So we have to deny the yet uncomprehended process in the yet unexplored medium. And now it looks as if we had denied mental processes. And naturally we don't want to deny them.[32]

The "conjuring trick" of which Wittgenstein writes is the basis of the exclusionary or negative sense of the reduction as exemplified in Griffiths's homologous analysis of emotion, emotions, *and moods* (all taken to be, at bottom, complexes of basic emotions). For theorists of emotion, this hinges on the presumed identity of our basic emotions with their affect programs *as well as the identity of our mood of anxiety with an as-yet undiscovered anxiety system.* However, an identity that works well in the case of basic emotions does not work well in the case of anxiety. For one thing, we have not established an anxiety system with which to identify our feeling of *Angst*. In addition, the plausibility of this presumptive anxiety system will depend, I would think, on the boundaries of the spatiotemporal field within which the validity of *Angst* is assessed.

In the case of the basic emotion of fear, placing the field's boundary near the skin of the organism for the observation of a brief event does not impair the empirical work to be done. But what is the empirical basis for Griffiths's expectation that moods as well as basic emotions ought to be contemplated as biological homologues within the boundaries of the individual's cranium? Griffiths's one-size-fits-all-emotional-phenomena theory appears to hinge on his psychological interpretation of primate behaviors: "Threat displays in chimps look very different from anger displays in humans, but when their superficial appearance is analyzed to reveal the specific muscles whose movement produces the expression and the order in which those muscles move, it becomes clear that they are homologues of one another."[33] From this Griffiths concludes, "The same is almost certainly true of the neural mechanisms that control these movements."[34] For his "deep" explanation of (mood as well as) basic emotions, Griffiths refers us further to the study of homologous pro-

32. Wittgenstein, *Philosophical Investigations*, section 308.
33. Griffiths, "Emotions as Natural Kinds," 238.
34. Ibid.

cesses in the brains of human beings and in the brains of rats. For this he draws on the "widely accepted account of fear processing" by LeDoux.[35] Leslie Brothers, a research neurologist, elaborates:

> LeDoux's research involves an experimental setup in which a tone is played to a rat in a cage, signalling (sic) an electric footshock to follow. When the rat learns the predictive nature of the tone, it shows typical defensive signs simply upon hearing the tone. This is called the 'fear conditioning paradigm.' LeDoux discovered that the conditioned response depends on a neural pathway which runs directly from the low-level auditory parts of the brain to the amygdala, bypassing the part of the cortex that is involved in auditory processing.[36]

She also maintains that, from a careful consideration of the data sought and obtained, "the footshock experiments are about rats learning to associate tones and shock,"[37] there is no guarantee that these experiments say anything about anything in addition. It is significant that clinical data gathered from animals with this neural pathway disabled indicate that the animals nevertheless experience anxiety.

At this point, I would like to ask if it is legitimate to equate rat anxiety with human *Angst*. Suppose, on the emergentist hypothesis, that this mood of *Angst* emerges from my brain. Under what conditions does the mood emerge? To be sure, my brain must be of a certain structure and complexity. I need Griffiths's biological homologues and the rest of my neurology as well. I will say that, in addition to my neurobiology, my interaction with others is a necessary condition for this emergence. This interaction entails language, I would think. Perhaps language is *the* major condition for my having this mood. The use of language depends upon a suitably complex brain. My point here is that neither my neurology *nor my social immersion over time* are dispensable. So, the emergence of *Angst* or any such mode of consciousness depends upon social interaction. This social interaction is thus a necessary, a priori, transcendental condition. Now the issue becomes a matter of the advisability of failing to keep in mind some of these necessary conditions for a science of moods. In a word, human *Angst* cannot be studied as the phenomenon

---

35. Ibid.

36. Brothers, *Mistaken Identity*, 54–55.

37. Ibid., 55. See also John Horgan's interview with LeDoux in Horgan, *The Undiscovered Mind*, 28–32.

it is apart from its emergence in the field of social interaction and linguistic concourse.

There is no need to speak about a rat's *Lebensform* in order to conduct a lab experiment on the basic emotion of fear, but I would suggest there is such a need for experimentation regarding anxiety in light of my social field, emergentist hypothesis. Brothers concludes that experiments such as LeDoux's experiment with rats "seem to prove what we already believe—namely, that emotion is a natural, biological part of ourselves. They pull our attention away from the fact that 'emotion' simply designates a set of shared social practices."[38] In my concluding chapter, I shall address the social construction aspect of *Angst,* but here I would just say that I do not suppose that an explanation of a basic emotion of fear requires much more structure than the affect program within the organism and a minimal interaction, not with an entire social context, but merely with a ready to hand object to occasion the fear response. So, let me return us to the matter at hand, the high-level performance of *Angst* and its quasi-intentionality.

For a suitable empirical study of such a richly intentional mood, a larger spatiotemporal world is required than that which is available within the skull of an individual. On this score, Daniel Dennett utterly, or perhaps ironically, subverts Wittgenstein's position mentioned above by taking Wittgenstein's warning against conjuring mental processes as a challenge to explain mental processes so thoroughly that they cannot be discounted. Dennett, an eliminative materialist, says of this *Investigations* passage, "As 308 makes clear, if we are to avoid the conjuring trick, we have to figure out the 'nature' of mental states and processes *first.*"[39] Wittgenstein, however, is doggedly insistent that philosophy ought to do its work at the level of the phenomenon and eschew the "conjuring trick" of simplifying what is the case in an appropriate context to what reductive theorists imagine ought to be the case.

It may be objected that there is something regressive in employing an analytic philosopher to make a case for a neuroscientific study of human anguish, but let us consider a lesson from Wittgenstein on the research significance of our human form of life, just as we took a lesson from Heidegger on the significance of our being in the world. Wittgenstein consistently denies and even ridicules all efforts to reduce

---

38. Ibid., 55–56.
39. Dennett, *Consciousness Explained,* 462.

what is shown and known in our human life or *Lebensform* to exclusively private, interior processes. While it would be anachronistic to see Wittgenstein as a participator in a debate on twenty-first century affective neuroscience concerning basic emotions and moods, I do consider mine a defensible interpretation of Wittgenstein's writings. At a minimum, I consider it worthwhile to propose an alternative reading of Wittgenstein on this matter of a field or background necessary to comprehend our emotional feelings—an alternative, that is, to the reading Searle has offered. I shall pursue this at some length in the next chapter. On my reading, Wittgenstein consistently resists the effort to reduce the field of consciousness to the brain of an isolated, essentially Cartesian subject.

As to the reduction of feelings, sensory and emotional feelings alike, to private brain states, Wittgenstein is unmistakably opposed to *tout court* reductive explanations. In *Zettel*, a posthumously published collection of notes that he likely wanted to include in his *Philosophical Investigations* but could not fit, Wittgenstein observes, "No supposition seems to me more natural than that there is no process in the brain correlated with associating or with thinking."[40] This appears to be mere hyperbole until we amplify his statement to read something like this: "No supposition seems to me more natural than that there is no process [wholly explainable in terms of processes exclusively *with-*] *in* the brain correlated with associating or with thinking." I am prepared to grant that Wittgenstein is, at the same time, hyperbolically moving beyond the bounds of my dissertation by urging us to attend exclusively to the extra-cranial, social world even to the virtual exclusion of our human neurology. So, I shall take this statement not as a denial of the necessity of affect programs or neuroscience in general but simply for its objection to the penchant for treating neurophysiology as the necessary *and sufficient* cause of all dimensions of all forms of our human consciousness.

To this end, Wittgenstein points out that it would be impossible to obtain a read-out of human thought processes from an individual's brain processes in the absence of an overall system (analogous to what I have been calling the "field of consciousness" that is necessary for the emergence of *Angst*) linking the one process with the other. It is just as plausible he says, still speaking hyperbolically, that our thought processes erupt out of chaos. An appropriate analogy would be the alleged material correspondence between a temporally frozen seed and a mature, thriv-

---

40. Anscombe and von Wright, *Ludwig Wittgenstein*, paragraph 608.

ing plant. There is no systematic material correspondence between the seed and the living plant that comes from it. Here Wittgenstein offers us something of a Zeno's Paradox in support of Heidegger's philosophy of *In-der-Welt-Sein*. There is, to be sure, an historical relationship between a certain type of seed and a certain type of plant that the seed produces, but there is no material one-for-one, this-to-that identity of parts within *this* here-and-now seed as such with parts of *that* plant months later such that we are entitled to infer the living plant from what is contained within the seed alone. So too it is impossible to determine what it is to be a thinking person (whose consciousness is, after all, intentional, in the world, and no Cartesian dream) working from the mapping of brain processes and neural events as if the subject ever existed apart from the natural world. A larger field (larger *temporally as well as spatially*) is required for proper analysis.

Now, within the biological system or background of the entire earth and its seasonal progressions that (historical) relationship between seed and mature plant can be comprehended. In turn, Earth's biosphere is comprehensible within the wider universe of axial inclination and orbital proximity to a given star, within a universe of time and space, within being. But if we were to take the interior of the seed at a frozen moment in time as the sole scientific field of endeavor, the plant would be incomprehensible. Not incidentally for the scientific endeavor, on such a restricted study of the natural phenomenon, no further horizons would be opened for scientific investigation.

To reiterate this point in terms of Griffiths's type of neuroscience: it is not that the homologies have no bearing on our emotional feelings; it is rather that the shared internal structure, or indeed any happening within the skin of an organism, cannot by itself account for the intentionality of *Angst*. Indeed, affective neuroscience has found that it cannot provide us with evidence of an anxiety system within the brain. As Panksepp explains, "The abundance of animal models, and the overall clinical complexity of anxiety indicate that we should be cautious in simplifying the issues that confront us as we seek a definitive understanding of anxiety *within* the mammalian brain."[41] What is it that generates our inability to achieve a definitive understanding of anxiety? It is, per my hypothesis, the conduct of a particular sort of neuroscientific study of

---

41. Panksepp, *Affective Neuroscience*, 212. See "On the Varieties of Anxiety Systems in the Brain," 212–13. My italics.

anxiety or *Angst*, a neuroscience that confines itself to structures and events predominately *within* the mammalian brain.

Over the past three decades, there have been at least three proposals for the basic substrates for anxiety, namely, nonadrenergic arousal from the locus coeruleus,[42] serotenergic arousal from midbrain raphe cell groups,[43] and a hippocampal-septal behavioral inhibition system.[44] As Panksepp concludes, each of these theories remains controversial. There is an accumulation of contradictory data. Most seriously, from the neuroscientific standpoint, is the *contradictory data* from animals with these areas and systems experimentally damaged. These animals "with damage to the brain areas mentioned above can learn to avoid foot shock and continue to exhibit anxious behaviors . . ."[45] This raises the question as to whether we can account for *Angst* in terms of anxiety systems that we locate predominately *within* the mammalian brain. Perhaps, to put the matter more philosophically, it is a question of recognizing not just *a* cause for anxiety, but a more *complete* account of the causes involved.

The structure necessary to account for the intentionality of *Angst* is us in the world or universe as a whole, though it is undefined and not comprehended. Hence we feel our relationship toward it anxiously. In my first chapter, I spoke of the quasi-intentionality of a mood such as *Angst*. By this, you will recall, I was at pains to explain that I was not implying that our feeling *Angst* might possibly be analogized (or allegorized) as if there were some pseudo-intentionality to the experience. Rather, my point is that feeling *Angst* entails a more comprehensive intentionality than we are accustomed to speak of in neurological discussions of emotion. *Angst* intends everything together, the world, what is on the whole. As Heidegger has it in his Nietzsche lectures, as a mood it is "a sustained openness" that we have toward other beings and toward being overall. As a mood, then, *Angst* thus provides us an insight into our own kind of being, our higher-level, more-than-animal being. It is this comprehensive intentionality that accounts for the opening of one

---

42. Redmond and Huang, "New Evidence for a Locus Coeruleus Norepinephrine Connection with Anxiety," 2149–62. Cited in Panksepp, *Affective Neuroscience*, 213.

43. Graeff, Quintero, and Gray, "Median Raphe Stimulation, Hypocampal Theta Rhythm and Threat-Induced Behavioral Inhibition," 253–61. Cited in Panksepp, *Affective Neuroscience*, 213.

44. Gray, *The Neuropsychology of Anxiety*. Cited in Panksepp, *Affective Neuroscience*, 213.

45. Panksepp, *Affective Neuroscience*, 213.

horizon after another in our ongoing study of reality—a natural reality of which we are already part.

To phrase it somewhat differently, then, on the matter of moods and higher-order emotions, we could say that Griffiths misrepresents the complexity and "reach" of the relationship between mental events and our extramental environment. On this score, Rockwell says that today's neuroscience habitually mistakes what he calls "pragmatic causation" for what Rockwell refers to as "*compleat* causation": "For those who do neuroscience, it is highly effective to assume that brain events are 'the' cause of mental events. There is overwhelming empirical evidence that whenever a mental event occurs, something happens in the brain. Conversely, when something happens to the brain, it frequently has an effect on the mental events of the person who possesses that brain."[46]

It is his work with brain-affected patients that undergirds Damasio's identification of brain states with mental events, as mentioned in my previous chapter, where I observed that there is a mild question-begging character to his widely held and common-sense identification of brain (or brain and body) with mind. The under-interpreted character of this common-sense identification comes to light in view of sciences other than neurobiology that also study mind. "Psychology studies the relationship between behavior and mentality." AI research proposes other physical and system substrates for thought, linguistics studies language, which is always intentional—all are scientific ways of studying mind, which "indicates that we can no longer understand the mind by merely understanding the brain."[47]

Within each of these scientific disciplines, there is an understandable tendency to assume that the object(s) of its particular field of study is *the* complete cause for mental events, whereas they are expert at the scientific study of only the trunk, or only the tail, or only a leg of the proverbial elephant. As I have stipulated, Griffiths provides a neuroscientific account of basic emotions such as fear in terms (predominately) of homologous structures. But there is more to the story of the mind as comes to light in the hierarchical brain, with its higher cognitive emotions and moods. If we could not fear, we could not dread, granted. But it does not follow from this that dread is nothing more than an affect program. Following this line of thought, I am interpreting Griffiths as

46. Rockwell, *Neither Brain Nor Ghost*, 53–54.
47. Ibid.

being open to a fuller consideration of analogous structures and even to a version of social or cultural construction. Would it not be elegant in the neuroscientific study of moods, that is, would it not be more scientifically plausible to expand the boundaries of our concept of "mind" so as to include in its (that is, the mind's) structure the structure of the entire world?

Unlike Griffiths's present thesis concerning mood, Heidegger's admonition not to reduce or dissolve phenomena such as our experience of conscience or our feeling *Angst* to a predominately biological "explanation" is not primarily an admonition to avoid the faulty analogy and the mistaken identity between states of mind and brain states. Rather significantly, Heidegger does not want us to neglect the validity or significance of the phenomenon of *Angst* and thereby lose our ability to recognize our capacity as human beings or *Dasein* to be authentic and responsible selves. The lesson for us is that, on the basis of a thin or close-to-the-skin intentionality and a predominately biological, inside-the-cranium explanation of our feeling anxiety, anguish or *Angst*, our capacity to attend cognitively to our experience of conscience, which in turn rests upon the rarely-studied phenomenon of feeling *Angst*, will be dissipated. In a word, if the subjective phenomenon of *Angst* is thus discounted, the possibility for the subject to know herself as a responsible social being is forfeit. At the same time, the bar for the validation of the mood of anxiety is higher today than the bar was in Heidegger's time. That is to say, the validation of *Angst* that Heidegger argues for stands in need of scientific verification.

For Heidegger, whose existential analysis of conscience entails the validity of this feeling, *Angst* is "primordial," that is, fundamental to our understanding of our human being, which is essentially temporal. We know this because we feel *Angst* over the long term. In other words, our experience of *Angst* makes us what we are and thus in considering our anguish or anxiety indicates we learn who we are. *Angst* is an integral aspect of the kind of being that we human beings are as *Dasein*, a disclosive feature of our existence that exhibits our potential for being responsible individual persons. [48] As to the requisite verification of this, I have already suggested that rather than understanding our moods on the basis of our basic emotions, we can thus endeavor to understand our emotions on the basis of our moods, with a close eye on the issue of

---

48. See, for example, Heidegger, *Being and Time*, 249.

affective intentionality. The crux of the matter is this *intentional* aspect to our emotional feelings.[49]

Husserl, as is well known, allowed intentionality only to cognition. Heidegger opened a window on our self-understanding with his argument for the intentionality of moods, which are the feelings that they are and are not at all parasitic upon cognition, as Husserl supposed. I mean to do more than simply rehearse this twentieth-century development, however. Cognitive neuroscience is now at the point, I am saying, that it can begin to verify Heidegger's philosophical insight.

Throughout this chapter I have adopted a ground-up vocabulary in deference to the success of current affective neuroscience in analyzing basic emotions. Theoretically, one could just as well begin with the richly or comprehensively intentional nature of moods and come, by way of a subtractive or *via negativa* strategy, to a similarly neuroscientific analysis of the lower basic emotions, perhaps characterized vis-à-vis moods as relatively world-poor and minimally, almost incidentally, intentional. In any case, we do have this human experience of *Angst*, although it is not yet being researched as a mood but is generally construed in affective neuroscience as a complex of basic emotions.

As we have seen, Heidegger teaches us to beware of dissolving the phenomena of our various moods with hasty or *immediate* scientific explanations. This is hardly a dismissal of neuroscience. Only if we acquiesce, along with "the they," and grant that verification almost exclusively in terms of the individual's neurobiology is the gold standard for all topics of affective neuroscience—only then are we led to see higher-level feelings to be merely perspectival qualia,[50] idiosyncratic aspects of one person's consciousness and therefore as something unreal, dissolute, shallow—a "mere whisper" of epiphenomena, as Irvine suggests. But this is a concession that existential, phenomenologically minded continental thinkers such as Heidegger do not grant.

Nor, by the way, do existential, analytic philosophers such as Wittgenstein. Perhaps affective neuroscience is, for example in the case of anxiety, now ready and open to reconsider the viability of brain sys-

---

49. For the definition of a feeling as "an emotion considered in abstraction from its intentionality" cf. de Sousa, "Emotional Truth," 247–63, 247.

50. Dennett, *Quining Qualia*. Dennett argues for the elimination of the notion of qualia altogether. But he does so on the assumption that these feelings are detachable from their intentionality.

tems to account for the phenomena of higher emotions or moods. The hypothesis that mind is best construed as a nexus of brain and body and world offers the best promise, I am saying, of studying distinctly human emotional phenomena scientifically.

In other words, on the emerging neuroscientific hypothesis that mind is not merely brain or brain-plus-body, but is in fact best construed as a nexus of brain-body-world[51] or as Heidegger has it, as *In-der Welt-Sein*, we can speak of validating a mood or feeling within the field or structure of the world as a whole, including, but not limited to, the individual organism.

In the final analysis, a feeling is felt subjectively, of course, but it cannot ultimately be validated in our day and age on the basis of how keenly it is felt or how poetically it is described. Rather, a feeling is validated objectively, that is, it is made amenable to scientific verification, on the basis of its intentionality. A feeling or mood is what it is subjectively (it is a property of human consciousness with a first-person ontology), but it is verified scientifically by our neuroscientific contemplation of its intentionality. Our neuroscientific contemplation leads to the study of this feeling in terms of a social field. The more comprehensive the object of the feeling, the broader its meaning. This significance is due, as I have been arguing, not to the intensity of a merely subjective feeling, but to the objective comprehensibility of the object of that feeling.

SUMMARY

Angst intends the world or, as Heidegger has it, its object is "what is on the whole" (*Sein im Ganzen*). The project therefore is not to evaluate the feeling *qua* feeling, as if "feeling" here is a thing in itself and therefore denotes an item in one's brain or body, that is, a subjective quale, or a neural event that is, itself by itself, a feeling. Instead, my point is to emphasize the question as to *what* we feel when feeling, or what the mood is all about. Affective neuroscience has been successful in its analysis of basic emotions with little attention needing to be paid to the intentionality of these emotions, such as fear, but remiss in its consideration of the role of intentionality for other kinds of feelings. On this basis, I am calling for an "affective neuroscience-plus." Emerging neuroscience, such as that articulated by Rockwell—a neuroscience that is open to complete

---

51. Rockwell, *Neither Brain Nor Ghost*, 21–36.

causation and thus open-minded in its construal of mind as a nexus of body, brain, and world—is suitable for such an objective verification of higher-level emotional feelings and moods. This amounts, roughly, to showing that feelings are genuinely intentional in the way beliefs and desires are, *assuming that we can achieve a sufficiently broad neuroscience.* Last-generation neuroscience, with its reductive paradigms of brain as mind or of an individual organism's brain and body as mind, is inadequate to the task on account of its presupposition of what Rockwell calls Cartesian materialism, that is, its penchant for confining its field of theoretical explanation to within the brain of the individual.

My intentional argument thus far may strike some readers as a continental commentary on affective neuroscientific theory. Perhaps these readers, familiar as they are with Searle's popular works on intentionality, are willing to concede pro-tem that my critique has some plausibility in regard to neuroist reductions of *Angst*, but nevertheless await what might be thought of as a more analytic (or somehow more *neurological*) version of my intentionality thesis before they can consider the validity of my thesis that we can verify our feeling of *Angst* in intentional, objective terms. If anxiety cannot adequately be verified in terms of current affective neuroscience, then can it be verified neuroscientifically? Continuing my argument that *Angst* is amenable to a broader type of neuroscientific verification leads finally to a consideration of its verification in social neuroscience. The case for verifying this mood by means of *social* neuroscience is the central concern of the following chapter.

THREE

How the Mood of *Angst* Might Be Verified Empirically

> We have no evidence whatsoever that what happens in the brain can create conscious experiences all by itself. Consequently, it seems sensible to conclude that the supervenience base for all mental events, including subjective experiences, includes not only brain events, but events in the rest of the body and in those parts of the environment with which the conscious organism maintains a synergetic relationship... "Behavioral field" is not a mere metaphorical extrapolation from other kinds of field theories... If the science were in place to quantifiably study how such a field radiates outward from the organism into its environment, there would be no reason to dismiss such studies as mere mystical claims that we are "one with everything." On the contrary, this behavioral field would be our best scientific approximation of what mind is identical with.
>
> —W. Teed Rockwell, *Neither Brain Nor Ghost*[1]

IN THE PREVIOUS CHAPTER, we saw that anxiety or anguish cannot be adequately described within a "nothing but" type of neuroscience, a neuroscience that is constrained to the cranium of an isolated individual and thus takes human anguish to be nothing but a complex of affect systems. The main reason for the failure to explain the mood *Angst* as nothing more than an alleged "anxiety system" is that the biological components that are the mood's substrate (Griffith's homologous structures, for example) are particles or modules in need of a connecting system of some sort. But the biological nodes (which may, it turns out, be as much hormonal as neuroelectrical)[2] do not themselves comprise the required

---

1. Rockwell, *Neither Brain Nor Ghost*, 206.
2. Ibid., 39–44.

connections with realities beyond the cranium or outside the skin of the organism.

Recognizing that there is deep disagreement about how biology can account for intentionality—indeed, as to *whether* biology can account for intentionality—I am here seeking a middle course, one that is not reductive to simple biology (Cartesian materialism) nor embracing of a full-blown substance dualism (Cartesian dualism). My approach is intended to be compatible with a kind of naturalism about the mind. What is distinctive about this middle course I am beginning to chart is that my concept of "mind" has extra-cranial extension. It is also true that I am speaking almost exclusively about "mind" and "consciousness" in the narrow sense of "affect." In their wider sense, "mind" and "consciousness" include cognition and volition as well, but my concern is with affective intentionality. "Rationality" embraces cognition, volition, and affect alike. My thesis calls for the inclusion of affect within our concept of rationality. A significant outcome of this extension of "mind" is that the scientific study of affective intentionality is not restricted to the study of the brain in isolation from its embodiment *not only within the human organism but also within the world*. Recall from the previous chapter that I am construing mind as a nexus of brain-body-world. This is where Heidegger comes in.

In the first chapter, we saw that Heidegger, who was profoundly attentive to the *intentionality of moods*, recommended a field theory explanation. The aim of this concluding chapter is to unpack further Heidegger's abbreviated field theory vis-à-vis feeling and affection, particularly vis-à-vis *conscious* feelings, that is, emotion and mood, in an empirical manner consistent with the case for an "affective neuroscience-plus," such as I have begun to sketch out. My strategy is to address a recent analytic objection to my ostensibly continental argument for the neuroscientific verification of moods such as *Angst* in regard to our engagement with the world. I undertake this by seeking to translate what Brothers identifies as "the languages of mind and neuroscience"[3] into a common meta-language for the validation and verification of a mood. This meta-language is *social neuroscience*.[4] We could think of

---

3. Brothers, *Friday's Footprint*, 142.

4. The emerging study of social neuroscience is being defined as "the exploration of the neurological underpinnings of the processes traditionally examined by, but not limited to, social psychology" in order to begin, working from the standpoint of neuro-

social neuroscience as "a language of moods." Social neuroscience is a very recent development in neuroscience. Consequently, the manner in which a mood may be amenable to verification by social neuroscience can be discussed in a philosophical fashion. That is to say, it is appropriate at this stage in the development of social neuroscience to identify and even anticipate new conceptual understandings such as "mind" construed as the embodiment of the brain *in the world* that may be of use in the neuroscientific testing for emotional intentionality and hence in our understanding of the role of mood and lower-level emotions as well for us as human beings.

INTRODUCTION

Michael Luntley contends that in Heidegger's account of the primacy of moods as engagements with the world "mood is not a conceptually structured engagement," and that this "makes Heidegger an unreconstructed empiricist with all the traditional problems about the given."[5] His objection enables me to address in a preliminary fashion the question as to *where* intentionality is located. Is Luntley correct to imply that the intentionality of a mood is a primitive, unanalyzable "given" completely contained within the individual? An insight is often seen as an inner, idiosyncratic and therefore unverifiable given. So, is a mood nothing but an insight? I shall continue my argument that the intentionality of a mood is amenable to scientific verification within a suitable background, a field of consciousness inclusive of our intersubjective, emotional consciousness. This notion that the mind is best construed as a behavioral field or a field of consciousness is crucial to my argument. Because of this, I need to address in a more-than-cursory fashion the philosophical justification for such a field theory as opposed, say, to a connectivist theory that takes the mind to be little more than the brain or than the brain and body.

By "connectivist," I mean essentially Rockwell's definition. The definition has to do with the way receptor neurons are presumed to operate. Receptor neurons are described in signal processing terms as transducers that mimic input signals. "If all the neurons in the sense organs were

---

biology, "to understand the complex and dynamic relationship between the brain (and its related systems) and social interaction." See Decety and Keenan, "What Is Social Neuroscience." See also Wexler, *Brain and Culture*, 85–138.

5. Luntley, *Wittgenstein*, 122.

receptor neurons that functioned as transducers, and all of the interneurons [that is, *all* the neurons involved in the transmission of the perceptive signal] were in the skull cavity, the brain could be seen as the sole seat of cognitive activity . . ."[6] But does this connectivist assumption test out neuroscientifically in the case of affects?

As Rockwell points out, it is not the case that all or most of our neurons function as transducers. Taking visual perception as a case in point, the only transducer neurons are in the cones, which are sensitive to electromagnetic frequencies. The remaining retinal neurons, namely the bipolar, horizontal, and amacrine cells, connect groups of rods and cones into networks that in turn inform ganglion cells. The signals sent by each dedicated ganglion cell to the cranial neurons are already interpretations of single receptive fields, typically about one millimeter in diameter.[7] This sort of recognition, acquired from rigorous empirical experimentation, does seem to suggest that a field theory (in preference to a connectivist or serial-wired neuron theory) suits the kind of investigation necessary for the study of moods with their inherent intentionality. Emotional feelings, such as moods, are, after all, perceptions.

The field will, naturally, need to be more than a restricted perceptual cylinder in order to account for the formal object of *Angst*, namely, the undefined world as a whole. The field also needs to be more than a region of proximate relationship; it needs to embody the self and that *about which one cares*. Furthermore, the field needs to account for more than cognition. It must, per the intentionality-of-moods hypothesis, entail affect or emotion as well.

One way of parsing the difference between cognition and affect or mood in such a field might be to research the impact that anxiety has on a cognitive process, say, in the case of visual and spatial memory.[8] Stipulating that "the right prefrontal cortex plays a critical role in the distributed neural circuitry instantiating anxious arousal,"[9] the interaction between anxiety and cognition can be studied, according to "Anxiety Disrupts Visuaspatial Working Memory." If, that is, specific methodological desiderata are met. Among these criteria is the use of psychophysiological measures—in preference to self-reporting measurements—that

6. Rockwell, *Neither Brain Nor Ghost*, 23–24; also 156–59 and 183–88.
7. Dowling, *The Retina*, cited in Rockwell, *Neither Brain Nor Ghost*, 24.
8. See Shackman, "Anxiety Selectively Disrupts Memory," 40–61.
9. Ibid., 40.

are "sensitive to a combination of valence and arousal."[10] The valence, I would think, entails a sensitivity to the wider field in which the affected person resides. We could also speak of this field being "modulated by the emotional content"[11] of human actions, as long as we keep in mind that moods (in contrast to the basic emotions) modulate at a lower frequency. But the fundamental point here is to see the mind as "a field of purposive activity radiating into an environment rather than as a piece of biological stuff with a permanent border, size, and weight."[12]

As further prologue to my discussion of the neurological aspect of such a field theory of moods, let me address a related procedural or methodological difficulty exhibited within the objection against the structure of moods that we have begun to consider. The force of Luntley's objection that mood is not a conceptually structured engagement but only an intuition derives from a presumptive incommensurability between the language game of (1) the natural sciences (which seek the verification of a mood predominately on the basis of imaging the neurology of the human as an individual organism) and of what we may think of as (2) the traditional philosophy of mind (which seeks the validation of a mood almost exclusively by means of conceptual analysis in order to secure for mood a role in human rationality).

In order to elaborate on Heidegger's abbreviated field theory, I shall first enlist Wittgenstein's concept of the background, which I see as another philosophical argument for an implicit field theory in respect of our feelings, in particular, in respect of our emotional feelings. This will lead next to my critique of Searle's use of the background in his version of social constructivism[13] since Searle reduces Wittgenstein's field theory of background to a biological "Background," which is quite insufficient for the task of verifying or scientifically testing a mood. The problem with Searle's background theory in brief is that it depends upon a connectionist or, in other words, on a serially-wired-neurons model. But first, how, exactly, shall we move on from here? Which "language game,"

---

10. Ibid., 42. See "Methodological Desiderata for the Study of Affect X Cognition," 41–43.

11. Chouchourelou, "The Visual Analysis of Emotional Actions," 63–74. See esp. 63–65 for mention of emotional modulation.

12. Rockwell, *Neither Brain Nor Ghost*, 77.

13. For which see Searle, *The Construction of Social Reality*, 127–47. See also Searle, *Mind, Language, and Society*.

that is, scientific language or a phenomenological vocabulary such as we acquire from Heidegger, is appropriate for our current investigation into the mood *Angst*? To speak in a rough and ready fashion, what is needed is a way to speak the continental, phenomenological insight of Heidegger, namely, that moods have intentionality, in the analytic, scientific idiom of our century. For this reason, we turn to the promise of social neuroscience as a *lingua franca* for affective intentionality. This will be our procedure. On to the empirical testing of an initial continental hypothesis.

The presumed incompatibility of natural science language (1) and the so-called "language of mind" (2) notwithstanding, it is one thing to offer a philosophical and even a preliminary scientific critique of a connectivist and predominately biological account of moods, but it is another to argue for a field theory of mood. How can we progress from Heidegger's recognition of a mood's intentionality beyond the analysis of moods in current affective neuroscience? Well, we can see how the common language of social neuroscience might provide a suitable means of verifying a mood in terms of its noncognitive and nonvolitional *affective* intentionality located within the field of our social and linguistic background. The question we are now after is, "What sorts of things happen to the neurological substrata that explain how emotions are intentional?" We are moving on to a scientific consideration of this intentionality thesis in a *social* neuroscience in view of our human kind of being in the world. This being-in-the-world is, of course, much more than an accident of geography, but rather expresses an *Existential,* that is, a necessary, essential, required definitive statement about human being. As we saw in the previous chapter, this is what Rockwell, Brothers, and others have argued against the dominant trend. It is their work that constitutes, in light of the demands of my intentionality thesis, the best trend in neuroscience today and thus paves the way for the empirical study of moods in social neuroscience, as I elaborate below.

ENVIRONMENT AS *UMWELT*

A few years ago, the professor who introduced me to Heidegger observed in a department colloquium that a charitable person might say "that analytic philosophy is characterized by being both rigorous and uninteresting, whereas the continental variant has its distinguishing traits in being interesting and nonrigorous." Taking Professor Ibañez-Noë's observation at face value, it seems to be both fair and salutary to submit the "interesting continental" concept of *Angst* (and my intentional analysis of this mood) to a "rigorous analytic" analysis. Not to overstate the contrast, of course, as thinkers who would hardly be labeled as "continental" have written extensively on intentionality.[14] We may also agree that the "Berlin Wall" between European and Anglo-American thought is largely dismantled. But mention of a contrast between Heidegger and contemporary "analytic" thought allows me to highlight the contrast between connectivist theories (the "serial neuron" view briefly noted above) and "nothing but biology" theories which, it seems to me, fail to consider affective intentionality as an irreducible intentionality on the one hand and, on the other, a field theory of mood that ought to yield one manner in which affective intentionality can be tested out.

"Tested out"—that is, neurologically, but understanding that our neurology is providing evidence of what we used to refer to as *adaequatio*, our fittedness, our connaturality, our natural attunement to the world as our environment. "Tested out" neurologically also in respect to our ongoing engagement with our world. Whereas Kant argued that spatial and temporal categories are a mind-supplied condition of knowledge, my argument is that we are spatiotemporally situated not simply, perhaps not even fundamentally, on the basis of our cognitive performance but on the basis of our emotional being. It may be objected that I have just reverted to a continental vocabulary where most contemporary theorists would require a natural science explanation instead. This is a further reason for me to engage with a recognized analytic objector to the meaningfulness of moods.

In order to be certain that this analysis is relevant to the topic of mood as we approach topics in philosophy of mind today, let me take up at some length the objection to Heidegger's concept of mood as expressed in a recent book by the Wittgenstein scholar Michael Luntley. To provide a context for his objection, in a footnote to his discussion of the rules or normative patterns of correct linguistic usage by which we engage with our world, Professor Luntley writes, "From what I know of Heidegger, the primacy of the concept of mood in his account of our fundamental engagement with the world leaves the question I am asking unanswered."[15] His analysis of our bodily relations to the world, which

---

14. For example, see Dennett, *The Intentional Stance*.
15. Luntley, *Wittgenstein*, 122.

cannot fail to be amenable to rational investigation, takes place within what Luntley calls "the space of reasons."[16] He concludes his footnote with this objection to Heidegger: "Is 'mood' a conceptually structured engagement or not? I suspect it is the latter. If so, that makes Heidegger an unreconstructed empiricist with all the traditional problems about the given."[17] In other words, I take it that Luntley is skeptical of any role for emotions, which are noncognitive, in our rational apprehension of the world. By way of reply, we could ask whether our engagement with the world is exclusively cognitive, as Luntley presupposes. This suggests a brief consideration of what we mean by "the world" as we begin to appreciate the way or ways in which we engage with it.

How is our engagement with the world structured? Heidegger's term *Umwelt* seems especially fruitful. *Umwelt* emphasizes our felt relationship to the world in terms of its features that matter to us.[18] The operational definition of "world" as what-we-care-about seems congenial to a social neuroscientific verification.[19, 20] *Umwelt*, as an answer to the question as to what the world is, may then suggest to science-minded emotional theorists that our neurological or hormonal research might benefit from the hypothesis that consciousness entails intentional reach. We are, for example, emotionally conscious of our own somatic condition. We feel well or not about our bodies. Well-defined, nearby objects elicit emotional responses, such as the basic affect of fear. At the same time, we may indeed not even perceive nearby objects while attending to farther away, undefined formal objects. We feel *Angst* about the world on the whole and our place in it. Our emotional experience embraces a more-than-proximate field of consciousness. Accordingly, Rockwell explains that neuroscience would do well to adopt an operational understanding of "mind" not as brain, but as a nexus or field of brain-body-world. He writes:

16. Ibid., 111–12.

17. Ibid., 122.

18. For a fuller discussion of the role of *Sorge* or care in Heidegger, see Caputo, "*Sorge* and *Kardia*," 327–44.

19. See Rockwell, *Neither Brain Nor Ghost*, 90.

20. See Inwood, *Heidegger Dictionary*, 245–48. Inwood explains that there are three possible approaches to the question, "What is world?" "In the early lectures, Heidegger speaks of three co-ordinate subworlds: the *Umwelt* ('environment, the world around us'), the *Mitwelt* (with-world, 'the people about one') and the *Selbstwelt* ('self-world, selfdom,' a precursor of the later *Dasein*)," 246.

> I do not believe that Reality consists of two fundamentally different substances, one mental, the other physical.... I'm saying that everything that embodies the mind is physical, but *there are also nonneurological physical items in the body and the environment which embody the mind*. The brain is *part* of what embodies the mind, but not the *sole* embodiment of mind. When people say that experiences reside in the brain, what they mean is this: brain cells interact in a certain way, and experiences emerge from those interactions. Consciousness is not an intrinsic property of brain cells; individual brain cells are not conscious. It is the interactive pattern between cells which produces consciousness. That is why it is in principle possible to replicate this pattern in some other substance, such as silicon, and thus create conscious robots.[21]

Simply put, brain cells do not account for their own motion. Their motion is not entirely self-caused but also world-caused. When we have experiences in the real world, the neurons are interacting in the shared world of one's body and one's environment. Just as sensory feelings are *of* the world or items in the world because they are caused by the extramental world and items outside our bodies, so too emotional feelings are *of* the world or items in the world because the emotional feelings are not self-generated. This is what I mean by referring to the "intentional reach" of *Angst*, for example. This intentional reach accounts for the world-embodiment or the being-in-the-world of brain and subject that I am recommending as an advance on simple brain-in-the-individual-organism embodiment.

In past generations, generations accepting of the Cartesian divide between inner mind and outer world, it was considered scientifically respectable to proceed as if there was a causal relationship reaching *from* the inner mind *to* the outer world. When the spiritual dimension of the Cartesian interface between the inner and the outer at the pineal gland was effectively deleted from the scientific and research models, there was no place left to serve as a spiritual hyperspace in which the genuine self could reside. Notwithstanding, science continued under the conviction that there needed to be an inner headquarters of the self. This need was filled with the paradigmatic assumption of an inner self residing, not in the immaterial soul, but within the material brain. This is what Rockwell means by "Cartesian materialism." But it is no longer plausible to see the

---

21. Posted correspondence by Teed Rockwell at http://forums.philosophyforums.com/thread/16866, no pagination (accessed 9/19/06). Italics added.

relatedness between inner and outer as a one-way street. As Rockwell says:

> Why then do I reject the idea that the head is headquarters? Because modern science no longer supports the view that the neurons outside the skull are mere message cables. The nervous system is cognitive all the way through, and the so-called brain is just that part of the nervous system that happens to be in the skull. I am not going to list the data I have to support that claim. It takes up all of Chapter 2 of my book [*Neither Brain Nor Ghost*], and there is plenty of other data elsewhere. There is also data in chapter 3 which gives reason to believe that the mind is also embodied by hormonal activities, and even occurrences outside the skin. . . . [P]roblems are starting to appear, and it seems plausible that a more correct theory may be needed to account for some of these anomalies, just as Einsteinian physics was needed to account for anomalies that couldn't be explained by Newtonian physics.[22]

Following Rockwell, I believe we can investigate neuroscientifically now whether the mere cognition of our body within the world accounts for our *being in* the world in a meaningful way. We ought to consider that a "meaningful" relatedness to our world is delivered, so to speak, not by our cognitive deliberations per se, but instead as our *felt relatedness*, that is, as a feature not of cognitive intentionality, but of affective intentionality. As a feature of affect, this relatedness to our world—this certainty that we are in the world—is an irrefragable aspect of consciousness since it is not mediated. We are in the world. We know this because we feel it. This is affective intentionality.

Included in the thesis of affective intentionality, then, is the proposition that mood situates us in the world and, further, that this felt relationship or affectively known being-in-the-world is the data of our conscious experience, of our fundamentally human way of being in the universe on which our cognition goes to work. As we are accustomed to hearing from phenomenologists such as Merleau-Ponty, physical proximity may account for the existence of (nonconscious) things in the world, but our human kind of being in the world is more than location on a Cartesian grid. "Where the scientist seeks the relations of things to one another common sense is concerned with the relations of things

22. Ibid.

to us."[23] So, in order to bridge the gap between the first-generation phenomenologists and contemporary theorists of emotions and moods, we have to translate the phenomenological insight of affective intentionality into the right kind of language for scientific experimentation. Bridging this gap requires getting over a deep-seated commitment to Cartesian materialism, however, as well as extricating ourselves from a concomitant commitment to the essentially *cognitive* rationality of the Cartesian ego.

Luntley's suspicion that Heidegger is an "unreconstructed empiricist" may be taken as an indication of Luntley's philosophical presupposition, namely, that only our cognitive structurings and *not* our emotional structurings are suitable for scientifically rigorous review. Thus, he would be reluctant to consider as part of empirical science how our affective neurophysiology both shapes and is shaped by *Lebensform,* our form of social life. Luntley takes mood to be irrational. For my part, I do not deny that a mood may be considered to be a "given." This is what differentiates an affect such as mood from cognition. Following Heidegger, I acknowledge that we are always in one mood or another and further that a mood assails us, that is, *moods are not cognitively constructed. But this does not disqualify moods as engagements with the world or even as rational engagements with the world. It is just that moods are a noncognitive form of engagement with the world.* With this acknowledgment of a mood's nonrationality, but not its (alleged) irrationality, we are in a better position to appreciate the scientific and philosophical appropriateness of investigating our emotional engagements with the world in terms of a field theory. With its place as a mood secured in human consciousness and rationality, our next concern is how to bridge the gap between a phenomenological validation of *Angst* as a bona fide subjective experience and a scientific, empirical verification of this mood's *intentionality.*

THE LANGUAGES OF MIND AND AFFECTIVE NEUROSCIENCE

Let me summarize how I am saying we can bridge the gap between Heidegger's continental insight regarding emotional intentionality and today's scientific conversation regarding emotional theory. The gold standard for the "language of the mind" (in the existential and phenomeno-

---

23. Lonergan, *Insight,* 181.

logical traditions), a philosophical precursor to the "language of moods," for which I am arguing, is conceptual clarity. Heidegger's first-generation phenomenology of mood excelled in detailed phenomenological narrations of human experience in terms of "keen-sighted popular speech," but was regarded by those fluent in the natural sciences as mere "folk psychology" (Paul Churchland). The language of the natural sciences (characterized for a time as "analytic" contra "continental") excelled in interpretations of painstaking laboratory experiments that portrayed human experience "neuroistically" (Brothers), often reducing *Angst* to incomplete biology-only explanations, the sort of hasty generalization presaged in Heidegger's caveat against "any psychological description" or "biological 'explanation,' that is, dissolution of this phenomenon."[24] All dramatic caricatures aside, we can challenge this presumed incommensurability between scientific and philosophical accounts of mood, given an overall account that gives due consideration to the intentionality of a mood as verified and tested by the neurology of social interaction (neuroscience). As I have said, the guiding question is, "*Where* is intentionality located?"

Well, as a point of departure for a common-language reply to Luntley, let us next take up his question, "Why could there not be calibration within subjectivity?"[25] as a demand for a suitably third-person verification of a subjectively experienced mood. Let us say that "calibration" amounts to the validation of a mood in such a way as to satisfy Luntley that a mood, if it is to figure in our account of rationality, must itself be cognitive. On this understanding, either a mood is a sort of cognition (which Luntley does not think it is) or a mood is invalidated, that is, is excluded from rational debate and study, inasmuch as it is an irrational something or other and thus is beyond the pale of rational inquiry.

But is Luntley's invalidation of a mood persuasive? No, it is not, for at least two reasons. In the first place, Luntley's dismissal of a mood from rational discourse depends upon an either-or fallacy, namely, "Either a mood is cognitive or it is irrational." There is a third possibility, the possibility brought to light by Heidegger, that *there is a role for something noncognitive in our account of rationality*. A mood is noncognitive. All the same, a noncognitive mood still plays an important role in rationality. As I have explained, a mood situates us in the world in a noncognitive

24. Heidegger, *Being and Time*, 248.
25. Luntley, *Wittgenstein*, 137.

and nonvolitional manner. We can take this as a validation, according to a phenomenological and conceptual examination of a mood's intentionality such as Heidegger provides. But I have also been arguing that such a (conceptual) phenomenology of mood is insufficient as a twenty-first century phenomenology. What is required in phenomenology today is not only conceptual validation but a certain level of scientific verification as well.

What I have been referring to as the (neuroscientific) verification of *Angst* must also, upon pain of irrelevance, incorporate a natural science account of the mood's *intentionality*. Cognitive intentionality is, we may say, a way out of having to see ourselves as potential brains in vats, but cognitive intentionality is not the topic of this book. My intentionality hypothesis has to do with *emotional* intentionality. In one respect, emotional intentionality just is a feature of the individual's emotional experience. "All experience is completely and irreducibly intentional."[26] It is, however, wholly inadequate simply to assert that *Angst* is essentially a subjective *quale* or that all moods are (merely) *qualia*. Exactly how, then, is it possible to advance beyond a conceptual discussion of a mood's intentionality to a more scientific verification of its intentionality?

If we can articulate a language of moods capable of contemplating the intentionality of moods and emotions in a neuroscientific manner, we ought to be able in effect both (1) to validate the intentionality of a mood as a noncognitive but nevertheless not irrational aspect of our human being and (2) to verify scientifically that this affective intentionality has a role to play in our rational appraisals—what Luntley refers to as the "calibration"—of ourselves in-the-world. There are scientific reasons for pursuing a more robust theory of emotions, one that takes serious account of their intentionality. What is at stake? Well, unless we can account scientifically for the intentionality of emotions, we will have to allow that we may be homologues in vats.

As I have explained, the physical components of our emotions or moods are pragmatic stances toward the world. That is, they are necessary but not sufficient causes of our kind of being-in-the-world, namely, human being. Luntley's worry is generated by his presupposition that the human subject is essentially cognitive. He fails to consider the validity of our emotions as unmediated engagements with the world. Nevertheless, emotions, a noncognitive aspect of our human being, have a role in

26. Rockwell, *Neither Brain Nor Ghost*, 17.

our account of rationality, as we have seen. My thesis is not a flight into continental idealism, but an argument for empirically demonstrating the viability of Heidegger's insight regarding the intentionality of our emotional being. I take Heidegger's position to be one of open realism. How exactly can we indicate scientifically that there is a demonstrable fit between our environment and our neurology? Let me carefully reiterate the philosophical framework within which we are looking for this scientific verification of Heidegger's insight.

In order to address Luntley's objection that the mood or feeling of *Angst* is not a conceptually structured engagement with the world and thus that this allegedly unstructured engagement renders *Angst* or joy or any mood an unsuitable datum for verification or "calibration," the reply I am insisting on is that *moods are not cognitions; nevertheless, they do structure our engagement with the world.* Moods do not represent our situation; they establish our situation.[27] Next, speaking parenthetically, we ought to expect a neuroscientific confirmation of this realization, but Professor Luntley's objection calls for an analytic and linguistic confirmation that we are moving in the right direction here, before I can elaborate such a neuroscientific confirmation. This invites a brief word regarding Wittgenstein's openness to the nonrational aspects of human being as well. I should mention that I am not pausing simply to address Luntley at more length, but in order to set the stage for a major objection to my thesis as seen in Searle's dismissal of affective intentionality, ostensibly based on Wittgenstein's concept of the background. Ultimately, I see Wittgenstein as both a philosophical critic of reductionist theories of emotional feelings and as something of a pioneer of scientific field theory concerning the human being.

This field theory has to do with what Wittgenstein calls "the background," which I see as one of depicting the field theory for our scientific inquiry into the intentionality of *Angst*. With "mind" now operationally defined as "a nexus of brain-body-world," and *Angst* recognized as a noncognitive but significant aspect of our rationality, we need as well an operational definition of the realm or field within which intentionality takes place. Wittgenstein's "background," if taken to be fundamentally our *social* environment in which we learn and exhibit our emotional

---

27. For a strong argument for the primacy of moods for cognition see Bollnow, *Das Wesen der Stimmungen*. My acquaintance with Bollnow is based on translations and synopses from Andrew Tallon (personal correspondence April–May 2006).

(and not merely intellectual) engagement with the world, fits the bill for just such an intersubjective, spatiotemporal field. Since much has been written lately about the background, in particular by Professor Searle, let us next consider carefully what Wittgenstein himself has in mind with his theory of human subjects who are more than cognitive beings and are constantly engaged with one another in a certain form of life against a social background.

THE BACKGROUND

What Heidegger accomplishes in terms of recovering a more comprehensive picture of the human being as *Dasein*, or the kind of being with an *Umwelt*, Wittgenstein accomplishes by exploring the supra-rationalist or noncognitive realities of human being expressed in the social intercourse of language. The things that we express in language and the features of human life (such as rituals and aesthetic sensibilities) that we express in language reveal, upon the kind of analysis evident in the work of Wittgenstein, especially after *Tractatus*, that the human subject is not exclusively cognitive. We do not do what we do and we do not know what we in fact show in language and in our conduct as the result of exclusively cognitive processes. Victor Krebs concludes from this that Wittgenstein came to regard the belief that cognition is our sole form of our relation with the world as what he calls "the stupid scientific prejudice of our time." I think we could say instead that Wittgenstein was aware of what I would call "consciousness diversity," as demonstrated empirically in our intersubjective uses and forms of language.

> When we conceive language as the product or instrument of an exclusively cognitive subject, then [language] is merely representational. . . . But Wittgenstein shows us that to a large extent in our ordinary use of language, and especially in our psychological language, it is many levels of consciousness and *diverse modes of knowing that are active beyond the rational*.[28]

Although it is coherent to refer to moods as being supra-rational, it is preferable to refer to diverse modes of consciousness, including affects and volitions, as being more than just *cognitive*. I have been maintaining that moods, as affective intentionalities, are hardly irrational and are thus undeserving of dismissal from philosophical and neuroscientific

---

28. Krebs, "Mind, Soul, Language in Wittgenstein," 2–3.

discussion alike. Our language, particularly our psychological language, is an empirical indication of the validity, that is, the natural fitness of human emotions as well for life in our world. In addition to language, neuroscience is an empirical indication of our natural fitness as emotional beings in the world.

This leads to a discussion of an "intentional field," an arena suitably inclusive to embrace all the factors—subjects in their world as well as brains in their bodies—that play a role in the neurology of emotional intentionality. Wittgenstein was alert to the need to see our human being as a dynamic system of activity. This attentiveness to the field of activity ought to make contemporary readers of Wittgenstein attentive to the reciprocal relatedness between one's environment and oneself within a field or a "web of meanings."

> In my psychological expressions I am participating in a system of living relations and connections, of a social world, and of a *public subjectivity*, in terms of which I can locate my own state of mind and heart. "I make signals" that show others not what I carry inside me, but where I place myself in the web of meanings that make up the psychological domain of our common world. Language and consciousness then are acquired gradually and simultaneously, and the richness of one, I mean its depth and authenticity, determines reciprocally the richness of the other.[29]

We ought, then, to acknowledge in a general manner that our shared *Lebensform* transforms us as individuals through the web of meanings in which we are engaged in language. I am, though, contending here for a narrow demonstration of this transformation predominately within the realm of neuroscience. It seems reasonable to hypothesize that our emotions in our *Lebensform*, empirically known in the course of our interactive use of language and an element of consciousness as we have seen, bioform our brains in the process. Here again, on account of the prevalent assumption of Cartesianism, it is worth emphasizing that I am arguing the case for a study of the brain *in its social context*.

What would Wittgenstein make of this notion of a behavioral field as a scientifically apropos model within which to verify our sensory or affective feelings? His analysis of language is commonly interpreted as if Wittgenstein's concerns are exclusively epistemological. For example, we can read summaries of Wittgenstein's project which say, "Wittgenstein

---

29. Ibid., 4. Original italics.

goes further than Heidegger in laying out how to investigate the cost of our continuous temptation to knowledge."[30] But I would submit that Wittgenstein was in fact expressing his dissatisfaction with the presupposed Cartesian psychologies of his day, making him a potential ally for my proposal. His approach may be taken as a more scientifically sophisticated way of making a case for the study of emotional feeling within a behavioral field than is available in Heidegger.

The specific insight that moods, like other cognitions, are intentional is Heidegger's discovery, to be sure. But Heidegger seems content to make his case without articulating a role for scientific verification in the language of the natural sciences. I do not think it would be wrong to speak of Heidegger's antipathy toward science. Heidegger warns us against absorption into the world of "they" or the average masses, whereas Wittgenstein would like to help us to avoid enthrallment to scientific theories that keep us from "looking and seeing" for ourselves what our experience, including the noncognitive dimension of our human experience, really is about. Wittgenstein invites us continuously to investigate empirically whether we are getting it right, to validate our psychological thinking within the social reality of the world as it is. He does this in the discourse and experimentation that is part and parcel of the active engagement of our human form of life or *Lebensform*. Does Wittgenstein contemplate the *intentionality* of our cognitive or noncognitive human performances as a separate concern? I am not claiming that he does, only that he is of help in pointing out a way that affective intentionality, along with other aspects of our human form of life, can only be scientifically assessed, namely, against a suitable *background*, our social background as it is.

This grounding or wider field of human activity highlighted in Wittgenstein's work points the way for the right kind of empirical investigation, the sort of thing that Wittgenstein insisted upon, although neither he nor Heidegger had our present-day neurological science to turn to. Further progress in our day means following the type of brain-body-world investigation of a mood such as I am looking for in social neuroscience. We are, as I have mentioned, finally in position to begin to acquire an empirical understanding of what one social neuroscientist calls the "interindividual process" of our social form of life that "alters

---

30. Ibid.

the functional organization of the brains of the interactants,"[31] not by means of rational representation (an outcome of our cognitive capacity), but rather by means of our emotionally felt relationships with one another (an additional, irreducible form of human being).

Recall that although these emotionally felt relationships can be cognitively assessed—after all, this book is not a treatment of existential *Angst*, but is a cogent assessment of the role of *Angst* in human rationality—they are not themselves cognitions. This is a phenomenological discovery. All the same, conceptual clarity is not the end of the story regarding the intentionality of a mood any more than the biology of the human organism considered in isolation from his social environment is. After Heidegger, the next step in the story of affective intentionality was the step from early twentieth-century phenomenology into late twentieth-century neuroscience, but a further step is in order for us. This further step is into a wider scientific field of investigation beyond the cranium that is more and more open to us as we continue to stride beyond the constraint of Cartesian materialism on our research paradigms.

To summarize to this point, we can see the contribution of social neuroscience regarding emotions and moods as an advance over last-generation neuroscience by keeping a firm hold on Heidegger's discovery that moods are intentional and then posing the question of "location" in much the way that Wittgenstein would have done if he had our current brain and body imaging technologies available to him. The location question would, I am saying, lead us into a realm beyond the cranium in order to account for what happens within the cranium. The question as to the location of emotional intentionality would inevitably lead to a "reciprocal neuroscience." How does our neurology shape our felt relationship with the world? How, in turn, does our world shape our neurology along the conduit of this felt relationship? These are both neuroscientific questions.

What then is the "locus" of intentionality? *The location of intentionality is a field, the relational space between conscious beings.* This field is analogous to a gravitational field. The phenomenon of gravity is understood as gravity (rather than as an innate property of a given body) in

---

31. Wexler, *Brain and Culture*, 34: "Emotion is an interindividual process that alters the momentary functional organization of the brains of the interactants, configuring and activating certain multiunit functional systems and dismantling and deactivating others. Contagion is at the heart of emotion."

"the between," the region embracing the interaction of material objects. The gravitational field is not understandable (i.e., it is not available for scientific study) if the field of inquiry is restricted to within a singular material object. In the case of a mood's intentionality, the intentional field is not created by cognitive discourse; rather, it pre-exists and is explored via cognitive discourse. Nor does this diminish the reality of the mood's intentionality. Here is why.

If we were to revert from the scientific to the older continental idiom of intentionality for a moment, we would have to begin with a critical appraisal of Husserl's discovery that "the essence of consciousness is its directionality."[32] Husserl, Heidegger's teacher, writes in his *Cartesian Meditations* of a being-in as something intentional and further explains that this being-in is an objective sense. What he refers to as "the intentional relationship" embraces the relationship between consciousness and the fact that consciousness is *of* some object. Thus, it is through the process of interpretation that semantic or intentional structures are constructed out of nonintentional elements. In other words, "All perceptual acts, according to Husserl, have one dominant characteristic; they point toward, or intend, some object."[33] Whereas Husserl argues for the intentionality of the cognitive aspect of consciousness, Heidegger discovers the intentionality of the affective aspect of our consciousness. Thus, I have been arguing, for the most part in Heidegger's terminology, that intentionality is not only a feature of cognition (which, as I understand it, is what Husserl has in mind by "interpretation"), but is a feature of emotional feeling as well. In fact, emotional intentionality is an irrefragable aspect of our emotional feeling, as Heidegger sees it. A basic emotion such as fear is *about* the object of fear or "what is fearsome," just as a mood such as *Angst* is *about* the world as a whole. Thus, emotional intentionality is a given. There is, then, no need to question a mood's given-ness; there is only a need to verify or scientifically establish its location in public space. This entails a neurological, but not an *exclusively* in-the-head, empirical verification.

The "in-the-head" portion of the ontologically robust affective neuroscience that I am calling for includes nonintentional elements that are part of the intentional performance. These nonintentional elements are our neuron-architecture, our neurophysiology. From the

32. Natanson, *Edmund Husserl*, 85.
33. Ibid., 85.

fact that these elements are nonintentional it does not follow that our emotions are nonintentional. Once we can get beyond this fallacious assumption—having already extricated ourselves from the penchant to discount the role of noncognitive features of conscious experience from their role in our rationality—we see as well the inadequacy of Cartesian materialism for our empirical study of affective intentionality, as in the case of *Angst*.

Heidegger's terminology anticipates the experimental difficulties we generate for ourselves with an exclusively inter-cranial neurological model of mood. But it is Wittgenstein who suggests a way to construct a language suitably inclusive to provide a scientific verification above and beyond what I would call *qualia*-type testimonies as to a mood's intentionality. Recall Heidegger's notion of *Umwelt*. We find the resources needed to verify the individual's care for her *Umwelt* in Wittgenstein's term, *Lebensform*. Much as Einstein is reported to have arrived at his theories of general and special relativity by obsessively wondering what it would be like to ride on a beam of light, we can wonder in a *via negativa* fashion what it would be like to live without the intentionality given in our engagement with the world by our moods. Let us consider this at some length.

To begin this apophatic investigation into what it would be like *not* to experience affective *intentionality*, or not to have what we may call our "emotional or moody relationship" with the world, let me turn to a thought experiment. Following the thought experiment, I shall return to the matter of investigating the intentionality of *Angst* and moods within the field of behavior or field of consciousness in terms of social neuroscience.

DAMASIO AT SOLARIS

This extended thought experiment will help to elaborate my *philosophical* reasons for arguing that we locate emotional intentionality in the world, that is, in the natural world, which includes but is not confined to the individual organism with a suitably structured brain. Earlier I described my position as "weak emergentist." It is time to explain that, inasmuch as my project concerns affective *intentionality*, my view is not exactly that emotional intentionality emerges from our neurology or our neurophysiology *simpliciter*. No, I take the entire natural world, inclusive of our neurology and our intersubjective form of life, as the supervenience base for emotional intentionality. This supervenience base includes, then, as Rockwell has it, "not only brain events, but events in the rest of the body and in those parts of the environment with which the conscious organism maintains a synergetic relationship."[34] This explains the scientific role I see for *social* neuroscience.

At the same time that I am looking to what we may call the "inclusive language" of social neuroscience, I will need to note that it is too early in the emergence of social neuroscience to assess its methodological predilections. For example, Wexler's *Brain and Culture* was published while I was writing an earlier draft of this book. And so, it is possible that I may turn out to be guilty of a fallacy of accent. Perhaps, that is, I am looking for social neuroscience to be *social* neuroscience whereas it will turn out to be social *neuroscience*, with insufficient attention given to the *wider natural field* or *complete supervenience base* from which affective intentionality emerges. At the end of the day, my hypothesis that the intentionality of a mood can be verified by means of a suitable social neuroscience will be vitiated should social neuroscience turn out to be, in the end, simply another version of mind-as-brain neuroscience. That said, let us see if a thought experiment that abstracts our emotional neurology from emotional intentionality can lead to an appreciation of the scientific need for this wider natural supervenience base in emotional theory.

My thought experiment is suggested by a science fiction story, Stanislaw Lem's *Solaris*.[35] Lem's 1961 novel, the basis for a Russian and an American film of the same title, illustrates that an individual's interior neurological processes, absent a shared form of life, are not sufficient to account for the phenomena of moods and emotions. Let me summarize and briefly illustrate my scientific thinking from my previous chapter and this chapter thus far as prolegomena to the thought experiment.

As I have been saying, interior homologous structures of the mammalian brain and so on may be a necessary cause, but are not a sufficient cause for mood and its intentionality. I have identified moods as affects. Affects are nonvolitional and noncognitive but have a rational role nonetheless. We may say, then, that an emotion or a mood is rational. In this way affective intentionality is conceptually structured (it is not irrational) although not cognitively produced (it is affective, not cog-

---

34. See the epigraph to this chapter.
35. Lem, *Solaris*.

nitive). One element, the inner element of this conceptually structured engagement with the world—but not the entire field of consciousness or "mind"—is verified on the basis of brain imaging scans. For example, current empirical findings regarding "mirror neurons" capture one element of this intentionality. Becchio and Bertone have documented neurological activity that they were able to coordinate with various activities of both primates and humans. Their research led to the discovery that the same neural activities occur when a primate, for example, observed another monkey eating a banana, as when the primate itself ate a banana. Apparently even the contemplated activity coordinates with the neurological happenings that occur when the individual engages in that activity. This has led the mirror-neuron researchers to contemplate the hypothesis that such mirror neurons may account for shared intentionalities and emotions.[36] Such data open a window on the social background within which these neurological events take place over time.

By way of further possibilities, the authors of this study observe that "[i]t appears therefore that a whole range of 'mirror matching systems' may be present in the human brain. In other words, 'mirror phenomena' are not to be seen as limited to a particular group of motor neurons in the ventral cortex, but as a modality of functioning which is widespread in the brain."[37] They conclude, "[A]t a neural level the difference between individual and collective intentions [depends upon] the format of the underlying neural representations."[38] By such data, the social aspect of social neuroscience comes to the fore and the intentionality of emotions and moods is thus given scientific plausibility.

Although, as I have said, the neurology is not the complete cause to account for emotional phenomena, it is a pragmatic cause. Recall that a "pragmatic cause" is *a* contributor to the emergence of the phenomenon that is taken to be *the* cause for the phenomenon, often by specialists whose expertise is in the one type of cause. But one type of cause ought not to be taken uncritically as the supervenience base. The fallacy in this move is the assumption that, by declaring *a* cause with which one is familiar to be *the* cause, we constrain ourselves from taking into account all of the contributing factors that led to the emergence of the

---

36. See Becchio and Bertone, "Wittgenstein Running," especially "Sharing Sensations and Emotions," 130–31 and "Back to the Problem of Shared Intentions," 131–32.

37. Ibid., 130–310.

38. Ibid., 135.

phenomenon under study. The complete list of all contributing causes to the phenomenon would be its "complete cause" or supervenience base. A pragmatic cause for my writing this paragraph would be a reviewer's criticism of an earlier draft; the complete cause would entail as well my neurophysiology, my world, and our entire shared history. As to emotional intentionality, we can make the case for a science open to investigations leading toward the complete cause by seeking a dramatic way to loosen the intentional ties in order to see if we can even contemplate neurological research into an emotional feeling or a mood, absent the social space—the intentional, in-between field, as I have described it—of our form of life.

So, the evidence of mirror neurons suggests not our self-sufficiency, but our *adaequatio* for our ongoing, developmental participation as rational beings who are in the world, certain personal features of which we are hard-wired to recognize, anticipate, and rehearse cognitively *as well as to feel our relationship with emotionally*. But what happens if we prescind the emotional intentionality of this personal engagement with our world that we *care* about some items or happenings but not others? That is, what if we eliminate what Heidegger calls *Sorge* from one's being? Suppose that we create an entity that is *simul* an emotional being neuroarchitecturally but lacks the capacity to *care*. In effect, such an individual would be *emotion-intentionality disabled*.

Stanislaw Lem provides such an affective-intentionality-free entity for our consideration in his novel *Solaris*. The title entity is a planet. Solaris is a planet of a binary star, traveling in an orbit that appears to violate the laws of celestial dynamics. Its entire surface, except for a small number of barren islands in its southern hemisphere, is a colloidal "ocean" that is clearly alive and perhaps sapient. Although the purple surface of this colloidal "ocean" is chaotically restless, perpetually seething with fleshy foam, earlier explorers were intent upon discerning some sort of rational order in the midst of its metamorphoses. The Solaris "ocean" produced temporary structures of great complexity that suggested but ultimately defied typological classification. For example, wavelike ridges were vaguely classified as "extensors," city-like structures were named "mimoids," bird-like somethings that detached themselves and moved independently of the ocean body were tagged "independents." Colossal figures of babies and other human-appearing memes appeared.[39] While

---

39. See Stableford, *The Dictionary of Science Fiction Places*, 285–86.

it is clear that the planet may be said to be engaged with its universe rationally (it appears to be conducting innovative mimetic experimentation) as well as volitionally (under no coercion, it is doing whatever it wants to do whenever it wants to do it), it is nonetheless disengaged emotionally. Furthermore, this disengagement is long-term.

Someone may object that this disengagement is itself a mood; but it is rather the absence of mood. That disengagement is the *absence* of a mood, a disability, is indicated by the candidate moods from Heidegger and Wittgenstein, namely *Angst*, equanimity, and joy, which are all, by definition, engagements with the world.

Ultimately, resident scientists in a permanent exploratory station on the planet were visited by neutrino-formed instantiations of their deceased lovers and long-dead children. These instantiations, presumably formed by the planet-entity, talked with the resident human scientists, lived with them, and in the case of the neutrino-formulated deceased wife of the protagonist, expressed her love for him. The human scientist is Kris. The name of Kris's deceased wife is "Rhea."

> [Neutrino-Rhea says,] 'I have strange thoughts. I don't know where they come from.' [Kris, the human scientist narrates:] It took all my self-control to steady my voice and go on, and I found myself tensing for her answer as if for a blow in the face. 'They are thoughts . . .' She shook her head helplessly. '. . . all around me.' 'I don't understand.' 'I get a feeling as if they were not from inside myself, but somewhere further away. I can't explain it, can't put words to it . . .' I broke in almost involuntarily: 'It must be some kind of dream.' Then, back in control again: 'And now, we put the light out and we forget our problems until morning. Tomorrow we can invent some new ones if you like. OK?' She pressed the switch, and darkness fell between us. Stretched out on the bed, I felt her warm breathing beside me, and put my arms around her. 'Harder!' she whispered, and then, after a long pause: 'Kris?' 'What?' 'I love you.' I almost screamed."[40]

Lem's neutrino individuals acquired emotion as the consequence, not of their neuron-architecture per se—though the narrative details are lacking, we are invited to see them as microcosms of Solaris—but rather as the result of their ongoing existence as individuals *in the world where they* care *about specific other persons*. They have their being outside the

---

40. Lem, *Solaris*, 108–9, inserts added.

Solaris-brain and find themselves engaged with a world of others and relationships not of their own making.

Lem's story enables us to see how a solitary entity possessing the homologous structure for emotion or the capacity of affect programs can nevertheless fail to know its universe inasmuch as the individual does not care. Like the Point in the zero-dimensional region of Edwin Abbott's *Flatland*, Lem's Solaris, for all its cognitive capacities in respect to computational power and its force of will, forever lacks the "intentional reach" that comes from being in the world in the way that human beings are, thanks to their long-term moods and short-term emotions.

Neutrino-Rhea is, we are led to understand, a response of the planet to Kris's conceptualizations of his deceased wife. Neutrino-Rhea loves and is loved by Kris. A fragment of Solaris that breaks away from the solipsistic brain can achieve what the brain *solus ipse* cannot. The finite individual achieves emotional being not merely as a function of its own material constitution, but by virtue of its caring (affective) interaction with the wide universe of other conscious beings. As seen in this thought experiment, this caring interaction is *sui generis* and not at all parasitic upon cognition or volition.

Notwithstanding the emotional interaction of its neutrino offspring, the planet Solaris itself remains unaffected by affection in much the same manner and for much the same reason as that single, solitary inhabitant who constitutes the whole of *Flatland*'s non-dimensional universe is not affected by someone else talking to it. There is no felt relationship, no mood on which either entity can, even hypothetically, relate to anything outside itself. Solaris possesses emotional architecture but does not care to perceive its neighbors, its world. Insofar as it is care-less, it is not a being-in-the-world; it is a world unto itself. As Lem's narrator concludes, "We all know that we are material creatures, subject to the laws of physiology and physics, and not even the power of all our feelings combined can defeat those laws.... The entire human race had tried in vain to establish even the most tenuous link with [Solaris, the planet-entity], and it bore my weight without noticing me any more than it would notice a speck of dust."[41]

The connection between caring and perceiving is being addressed as well in social neuroscience. For example, it has been demonstrated that the superior temporal sulcus, a critical component in the visual

---

41. Ibid., 204.

detection of activity, is interconnected in a complex fashion with the amygdala, generally understood to be a hub for the processing of emotions.[42] This constitutes empirical verification of what author Amy Tan describes in her novel *Joy Luck Club* when a mother looks into the eyes of a daughter who long doubted her maternal love and says, "I see you. I have always seen you." More prosaically put, "the visual analysis of human action depends upon emotion processes."[43] In the case of higher emotions and even more so in the case of a mood, how we feel determines what we (can) see.

Next, let us suppose that Antonio Damasio was an astronaut exploring Solaris. Let us further suppose that the physical architecture of Solaris was that of a human brain writ large, so that astronaut Damasio could navigate the planet with the same familiarity that the real life physician Damasio navigates the human brain as a practicing neurologist. How would astronaut Damasio identify the planet's feelings as emotional feelings? Could he identify a planetary mood?

Antonio Damasio, as you recall from my opening chapter, construes emotional feelings essentially as somatic perceptions. "As I see it, the *origin* of the perceptions that constitute the essence of feeling is clear: There is a general object, the body, and there are many parts to that object that are continuously mapped in a number of brain structures."[44] He considers the more global somatic perceptions that are "continuously mapped" in unspecified brain structures to be the contents of our emotional feelings. "The *contents* of those perceptions are also clear: varied body states portrayed by the body-representing maps along a range of possibilities."[45] Perhaps astronaut Damasio could identify the mimoid and meme occurrences on Solaris or other planetary happenings there as mental events, but how is he to identify them as feelings or as emotional feelings, stripped as they are of their intentionality?

The formal object that physician Damasio contemplates is the body itself. It certainly makes sense for a neurologist to do this. Physician

42. Chouchourelou, "The Visual Analysis of Emotional Actions," 63. See as well 65: "Taken together, neurophysiological data support the existence of tight connections between the processes underlying the visual analysis of point-light defined action [abstractions of a moving primate body presented to the subject as points of light only] and the processes involved in *emotional recognition*." Italics added.

43. Ibid., 63. See the abstract.

44. Damasio, *Looking for Spinoza*, 87.

45. Ibid.

Damasio is in the business of examining and explaining the neurological aspect of our emotional being. But can neurology alone account for affective intentionality? If the claim is that it can, then we must observe that this is a neurologically sophisticated Cartesian materialism. Damasio's neurological explanation, it seems to me, is itself a call for a wider field of inquiry. For example, whereas other emotional theorists locate the self in the brain, Damasio locates the self essentially within the skin. Still, what he does not seem to take account of is the need for an external formal object in order to account for alterations in the individual's feelings—which are better understood as feelings of the person in the world, not simply as feelings of internal feelings.

In the case of the neutrino offspring, astronaut Damasio would have something to work on for his empirical investigations, namely, the neuron-architecture of the neutrino-offspring as observed over the course of their engagement with the world of Kris and the other resident scientists. The social interaction would provide a background within which to calibrate or somehow measure and chart the essence, the appropriateness, and the viability of the feelings of the neutrino-offspring. But this field of inquiry is utterly unavailable in the case of Solaris, itself by itself, a "brain" that lacks intentionality. In a manner of speaking, Solaris is of the world but is not in the world. It does not care. The planetary entity has states homologous to what we, *In-der-Welt-sein* as we are, identify as emotional states, but it is not processing or representing anything outside of itself. For this reason, Solaris does not have authentic emotions or moods. It follows that higher emotions cannot be construed simply as homologous all-in-the-cranium states. For the same reason, moods cannot be construed as mental dispositions based on their homologous structure alone.[46]

Thus, astronaut Damasio could measure the intensity, location, and so on of neural events within Solaris. He would also be able plausibly to suggest that given events are somatic indexes of joy or anxiety. But the

---

46. See Macquarrie, *Heidegger and Christianity*, 23–24. Speaking of his translation of *Befindlichkeit* in his translation (with Edward Robinson) of *Being and Time*, Macquarrie suggests that perhaps "affective state" would be a better translation. While Macquarrie speaks to the German term, I would suggest that "affective *disposition*" is preferable in terms of modern English usage since "state" here inevitably conjures "state of *mind*" for those of us who met Heidegger in the Macquarrie-Robinson translation. A markedly different English translation is needed in order to emphasize the emotional intentionality that is at the heart of Heidegger's revolutionary recognition.

scientific plausibility of identifying particular neural events inside the Solaris entity as emotional feelings derives from an analogy with physician Damasio's experience as a participant being-in-the-world, in the universe, in which he (Doctor Damasio) experiences the intentionality of his emotions in our social *Lebensform*. For the entity Solaris these events cannot be emotional feelings. Why not? Solaris is not in the world; therefore, its feelings cannot be feelings *of* formal objects. Rather, they are unidentifiable happenings, without a suitable background against which they can be indexed.

Now, as in the case of correlating the functional organizations of the brains of interactants in face-to-face socializing in the case of linguistic development—in which the neurology of infants is, if you will, bioformed over time—so too it may be possible for social neuroscience to offer a neuroscience of mood. Our thought experiment brings to light one reason that neuroscience requires this social dimension, precisely for the reason that Heidegger's understanding of a mood's intentionality suggests. The mood-aspect of our human being demonstrates that we are immersed in the world, that it matters to us, however undefined that world may be at present. Our neurology and our social being are interdependent. *A suitable science of mood, then, requires the careful study, not of either the neurological or the social, but of both within a common field.*

The need for such a common field has led Rockwell to argue for dynamic systems as behavior fields. On the strength of his observation "that many of the parameters that are arguably responsible for embodying consciousness are hormonal, rather than neural" in the third chapter of *Neither Brain Nor Ghost*, in tandem with the realization that accounts of the relationship of an organism to its environment can only be partial and pragmatic, never complete (the topic of his fifth chapter) he concludes, "We have no evidence whatsoever that what happens in the brain can create conscious experience all by itself."[47] This is not science fiction; this is an empirical, scientific observation. What, then, does the model of dynamic or behavioral fields mean for the scientific study, for example, of moods?

> Consequently, it seems sensible to conclude that the supervenience base for all mental events, including subjective experiences, includes not only brain events, but events in the rest of the body *and in those parts of the environment with which the con-*

---

47. Rockwell, *Neither Brain Nor Ghost*, 205–6.

scious organism maintains a synergetic relationship. At any given moment, there will be a distinction between those processes that constitute the subject and those that constitute the environment. But there is good reason to think that this distinction does not have a constant and enduring borderline.[48]

A solipsistic organism possessed of a structure homologous to an absolutely isolated human being, but unrelated to its environment, cannot be said to feel emotionally in any scientifically intelligible sense. On the reasonable supposition that the planetary entity in Lem's novel took the conceptions of the human scientists in residence as its own cognitions, we could say in addition that this isolated entity failed to relate to the conceptual structure of its environment inasmuch as all it could have experience of was its own "*in-*vironment," but without the possibility of testing this out. Is the Solaris planet located in the universe? Yes. It is in fact actively influencing its immediate environment. Recall that its orbit is violating the laws of celestial mechanics. But is the Solaris entity, affective-intentionally disabled as it is, conscious of its being in the world? There is no evidence in the story for this. On the contrary, what interests the reader (who is not affective-intentionality disabled) is the dawning realization that the application of ethical standards to this cognitively and volitionally powerful entity that nevertheless is *not emotionally conscious* either of the human astronauts or of its own avatars is impossible. Solaris is, to all intents and purposes, ignorant of its being-in-the-universe. Is Solaris, in a word, sentient? Not in the sense that it has feelings *about* the world. Cognitive intentionality (theoretically having the world in one's field of vision) is one thing; affective intentionality (caring about the world, face to face) is another. The planet can cogitate and it can act willfully, but this is not the same thing as being a *feeling* entity. This thought experiment suggests why a homologous structure, unless incorporated into a wider field or supervenience base, cannot be *the* cause of emotional intentionality.

Emotional homology does not provide a sufficient ground on which to verify or validate what I have called the intentional reach of moods or long-term emotional feelings, either to oneself or to others. *Pace* Griffiths, even though the identification of *the* interior emotional homologue for basic emotions may be appropriate (an identification that I have granted throughout), for higher emotions or for moods the

---

48. Ibid., original italics.

identification of the interior structure itself will not suffice. This is because of affective intentionality, a relatively minor feature of the basic emotions, but a significant aspect of a mood. Without due consideration of the items in the individual's environment with which the individual is concerned, there is nothing on the basis of which emotional feelings can be indexed.

Rather, in order to validate the worth of emotional feelings as a way of knowing the value of the world, the appropriate question is not "what organ, programming or structure accounts for emotions" or "where do emotions come from?" but rather "*where* are emotions to be located?" Yet this kind of question is imprecise given the hierarchy of emotions, from basic emotions up to moods that I have been assuming. A better formulation would be, "Where do emotions, in particular our more enduring moods, situate *us*?" In this more careful sense, then, emotions are emotions in social space-time.

Less dramatically put, more attention to our social situatedness leads us to a more social view of the brain. "By virtue of having shifted to a social view of the brain, neuroscientists have reached a new threshold. They are beginning to describe mechanisms that might be responsible for contagious and intersubjective behavior."[49] Thus social neuroscience is a scientifically viable theory of emotional feelings in terms of their intentionality. It is a neuroscience that takes account of neurology in terms of the world's power to shape our neurophysiology. This kind of emotional ontology—I do mean "ontology," our study of emotional intentionality, and am not referring here to what Heidegger would call the ontic or factual character of moods—entails a field or structure of human beings being *in the world.*

As my thought experiment illustrates, a field adequate for the empirical investigation of a mood cannot be arbitrarily confined within the skin (or within the planetary influence) of an individual organism. Indeed, without such a behavioral field—what Rockwell refers to as dynamic systems theory or DST—all the "various biological and environmental factors cannot be seen as a comprehensible system."[50] It also bears mentioning again, this time not in the continental idiom of a mood bringing one ground after another into the foreground, but in

49. Brothers, *Friday's Footprint*, 78–79. See also "The Shift to the Social Perspective," 66–79.

50. Rockwell, *Neither Brain Nor Ghost*, 206.

the mathematical-scientific idiom of social neuroscience, that "we must not forget that every dynamic system is itself part of a bigger system ad infinitum."[51] Seen in this way, the field theory for the verification of a mood such as *Angst* accounts for the revelatory character of the mood. It situates us within our world in a meaningful way. It does so over a longer span of time, allowing as well for reappraisals of our relationship with our world. With this scientific rationale in hand following the extended thought experiment, let me adumbrate the appropriateness of a social neuroscientific view of *Angst*.

TOWARD A VALIDATION OF ANGST'S INTENTIONALITY IN THE COMMON LANGUAGE OF SOCIAL NEUROSCIENCE

In the case of anxiety, this mood is revelatory of our temporal being. Earlier, I had quoted Jaspers as saying that Nietzsche had a tendency to speak "out of his states," meaning that we had to be with Nietzsche in the same mood or abandon all hope of following him where he wanted to lead us. Thus Nietzsche may be capable of profound descriptions of *Angst*, for instance, but cannot help in the project of *validating* the mood phenomenologically. Much less, as is expected in any twenty-first century phenomenology of emotion and mood, can Nietzsche provide help *verifying* the intentionality of a higher emotion or mood neuroscientifically. We may perhaps be intoxicated by Nietzsche's powerful prose, but what is needed today is a more scientifically minded account. I have already referred to Shackman's "Anxiety Selectively Disrupts Visuospatial Working Memory." This qualifies as a scientific account in its review of data concerning the impact of how anxiety interrupts the cognitive performance in which the right prefrontal cortex distributes mental resources. Further, this neuroscience entails the recognition of anxiety's long-term duration, in distinction from short-term affects and basic emotions. In the course of elucidating their case for researching anxiety in terms of its noncognitive—indeed, in terms of its cognitive *disruptive*—character, Shackman's research group argues that, as a constraint on inferences that may be drawn from neuroscientific experimentation, "the paradigm must be actually capable of actually eliciting *enduring affect*."[52]

---

51. Ibid., 205.
52. Shackman, "Anxiety Selectively Disrupts Memory," 42, italics added.

How the Mood of Angst Might Be Verified Empirically 93

Accordingly, the investigation into the locus of affective intentionality must seek the mood's complete causation in what I shall call "the twice-embodied brain" (meaning the brain embodied in the subject's body *and* the brain and body embodied, in turn, in the world), over the long haul, each (i.e., the person and her environment) considered as distinct entities, but within a common field. This investigation will entail our physical being, including our neurology and endocrinology, to be sure. But it will entail as well the structure that encompasses a "space" or, better, a *space-time* adequate to address the mood's formal object, the world as a whole, and our social being in its affect on our neurology. Now that we are thinking of our neurology as twice-embodied, we would do well to fortify our understanding of the ground or background by which we know this second embodiment. This fortified understanding of Wittgenstein's background turns out to be critical for retaining this hard-won recognition that our neurological anatomy ought to be viewed as nonintentional elements of an intentional performance, in this case, our mood of *Angst*.

Let us reconsider then what Wittgenstein would make of such a neurologically adequate structure or "background" within which our moods and their intentionality can be empirically verified. In order to do this, it will be necessary to reckon with a text or two from Wittgenstein, specifically to grasp his concept of the significance of the empirical subject and something of his understanding of our language regarding the science and psychology of the noncognitive components of human beings as embodied in this background. In so doing, we will further attune ourselves to his decidedly non-Cartesian view of our form of life in preparation for the contributions offered to our study of mood by social neuroscience. This survey will serve to further indicate Wittgenstein's deep affinity with Heidegger on this score. But, to reiterate: Wittgenstein tends to speak in the language of the natural sciences, whereas Heidegger does not.

In affinity with Heidegger, who maintains that feeling *Angst* requires a more-than-biological explanation and a more-than-behavioristic psychological description, Wittgenstein provides this note: "Misleading parallel: psychology treats of processes in the psychical sphere, as does physics in the physical sphere."[53] What concerns him regarding this mistaken analogy is that "seeing, hearing, thinking, feeling, willing, are not

---

53. Wittgenstein, *Philosophical Investigations*, paragraph 571.

the subject of psychology *in the same sense* as that in which the movements of bodies, the phenomena of electricity etc. are the subjects of physics."[54] While we would prefer to say that physicists study electricity itself and not "the phenomena of electricity," I think that we can accept Wittgenstein's analysis of the logical misstep involved in speaking of the science of physics and the science of psychology. The physics/psychology analogy fails inasmuch as the physicist does his work on what is objectively observable, knowing that what is observable *is* the (physical) "stuff" itself, whereas the psychologist does her work on what is observable in the behavior of the subject, which is *not* the (mental) "stuff" or emotional feeling itself. "You can see this from the fact that the physicist sees, hears, thinks about, and informs us of these phenomena, and the psychologist observes the *external reactions* (the behavior) of the subject."[55]

I would like to offer a more nuanced explanation as to why Wittgenstein is ill at ease with the ready identification of psychology and physics. The behavioral psychology of his day, although perhaps content to remain for the most part at the level of outward behavior, also sought or presumed there to be a deeper explanation of the individual's behavior, mostly within the "black box" of the individual himself. In contrast, the physics of his day was up to speed in its apprehension of field theory. After the advent of special relativity and in the heyday of Heisenberg, physicists were accustomed to speak, not of the inherent properties of things, but of *fields* of gravitation, weak and strong attraction, and so on. Wittgenstein, I am suggesting, realized the inappropriateness of a psychology of the human being that construed the individual as a substance possessing inherent properties on the basis of which its behavior could ever be explained. This is a lesson for contemporary emotional theorists as well. Empirical verification ought to proceed on the basis of a valid paradigm of our form of life.

Since we are speaking about Wittgenstein and language, let me cite a familiar example of the interdependence of our neurobiology and our social situatedness in the case of language acquisition. Language acquisition involves both (social) imitation and (brain) formation. The social neuroscientist Bruce Wexler observes these two aspects to acquisition of language, "development-shaping social stimulation" and "characteristics

54. Ibid.
55. Ibid.

of the brain itself."[56] In the first ten years of a person's life, the period during which a child learns to speak and to understand language with ease, there is a "plasticity of neural structures" that, at the end of this first decade, begin to change "so as to maintain the symmetry and parallels *between inner structure and outer reality.*"[57] In this space *between* society and neurology, we begin to see an indication as to where intentionality is located. This empirical mapping of emotional development is what I referred to above as the bioforming of the brain. The point here is that there is not a static, side-by-side symmetry between brain structure and outer reality, but rather that there is a dynamic forming of the brain's structure that is the result both of its inherent plasticity *and* of its temporally extended embodiment in the world. In a similar fashion, I am maintaining that emotional intentionality is the result both of our neuron architecture *and* of our ongoing engagement in the world.

The second characteristic (the structure of the brain) has particular significance for our neurological theories. "If the usual language areas of the brain are destroyed in early childhood, children can still converse, read and write." Citing the research and conclusions of neurologists and experimental psychologists,[58] Wexler observes that "[in most individuals the language function critically depends on the activity of similarly (but not identically) located regions within the left cerebral hemisphere," and further, that these regions "have a distinctive cytoarchitecture that distinguishes them from homologous areas in the right cerebral hemisphere and from similar areas in the brains of nonhuman primates." His conclusion is that this analogical neuroarchitecture "has profound implications for understanding the relationship between the existence of special areas of the human brain that have distinctive anatomical features and special human functional capabilities."[59] How do we know the functional capabilities of our brain? We come to know our cyto- and neuron-architecture by seeing what brains in fact do. The capabilities are

---

56. Wexler, *Brain and Culture*, 118. For the full discussion of which this paragraph is a synopsis, see 113–21.

57. Ibid., 118–19, italics added.

58. Namely, Kinsbourne, "The Minor Cerebral Hemisphere as a Source of Aphasic Speech," 302–6;
Bishop, "Linguistic Impairment after Left Hemidecortication for Infantile Hemiplegia?," 199–208; Zaidel, "Right Hemisphere Language." These are cited in Wexler, *Brain and Culture*, 284–85.

59. Wexler, *Brain and Culture*, 119.

known as the capabilities that they are by virtue of the regular way that they fit with happenings in (select aspects of) our environment.

As I shall discuss below, the particular responses, for example, the neurological responses documented in facial recognition, provide a testable indication of the "both (neurology) and (environment)" conditions for things to matter to us in our *Umwelt*. At this point, I am emphasizing the interdependence of our inner neurological architecture and the outer world. Wittgenstein is deeply committed to a philosophical analysis that takes account of the socially interactive subject as he is being engaged, refusing to accept the "nothing-but theories"[60] against which the theories of John Searle cautions us, theories of mind that fail to consider the subject as a living, dynamically involved social being. "The story has got around that there is no place for subjectivity in our modern conception of the world. . . . Wittgenstein's genius lies in the way in which he resolves what had looked to be a major flaw in modernity—the dismissal of subjectivity from the way things are."[61] It is this commitment to rigorously nonreductive analysis that enables Wittgenstein, for example, to elucidate his private language argument against the Cartesian paradigm of subjectivity, a view of subjectivity in which all elements of the subject's experience, including his deep, sustained feelings, are construed as if they originated and generally remain within the event horizon of his own will. Wittgenstein's famous argument against the possibility of a private language for our feelings and sensations is a case in point. But what exactly does Wittgenstein actually argue about the impossibility of a private language for our feelings?

In response to the anticipated objection "that human agreement decides what is true and false"[62] in regard to our feelings, Wittgenstein points out that "it is what human beings *say* that is true and false; they agree in the *language* they use."[63] But language, which exists within the common social space in which we can express propositions that can be judged true or false and accomplish so much more, takes place in a social field, that is, it "is not agreement in opinions but in form of life (*Lebensform*)."[64]

60. Searle, *Mind, Language, and Society*, 47.
61. Luntley, *Wittgenstein*, 151 n. 24.
62. Wittgenstein, *Philosophical Investigations*, paragraph 241.
63. Ibid.
64. Ibid.

For a further example, after a consideration of the distinction between the activity of describing methods of measurement on the one hand and reliably stating the results of measurement on the other,[65] Wittgenstein goes on to wonder if we could "also imagine a language in which a person could write down or give vocal expression to his inner experiences—his feelings, moods and the rest" in ordinary language, for private use only.[66] The presumed response would be that only the speaker herself would *know* her feeling of pain, for example, whereas others would need to *learn* or infer her experience from her verbal expression of it. But Wittgenstein relentlessly pushes the point at issue and thus helps us to avoid the temptation to confine our study to the interior of the person this way: "In what sense are my sensations *private*?"[67] It is either false or nonsensical, he points out, to say that I *know* I am in pain. Such a locution presupposes an artificial glass wall of representational cognition between myself and our shared social reality. This way of speaking is necessarily disingenuous. "Other people cannot be said to learn of my sensations *only* from my behavior,—for *I* cannot be said to learn of them. I *have* them."[68] It is noteworthy that Wittgenstein does not say, "Others learn of my sensations or feelings from my behavior whereas I simply have them," but that "[o]ther people cannot be said to learn of my sensations *only* from my behavior." What, then, does fully account for other people knowing our *feelings*—that is, for our sensate and emotional feelings? [69]

It is a matter not of knowledge but of judgment;[70] a matter not of epistemology or appropriate cognitive representations but of shared

---

65. Ibid., see paragraph 242.
66. Ibid., paragraph 243.
67. Ibid., paragraph 246.
68. Ibid.

69. For my understanding of the German *Gefühl* as a way of referring to physical sensations and to emotional feelings alike, I am indebted to conversations and correspondences with Prof. Claudia Schmidt of Marquette University and Prof. Phoebe Lawrenz of Michigan Lutheran Seminary.

70. This may seem to be what Robert Solomon means when he refers to emotions as judgments, but it is not. Solomon regards emotions as another kind of thinking, whereas my thesis is that our feeling *Angst* is not cognitive but rather is a prime datum for cognition, a basis on which cognitive judgments are made, an irreducible intentionality. For Solomon's position see, for example, his "Emotions, Thoughts and Feelings," 1–18, as well as his "Emotions, Thoughts, and Feelings," 76–88, and Solomon, *The Passions*, 251–88. The theory that emotions are appraisals or evaluations is also treated in DeLancey, *Passionate Engines*.

human being in our common world. By this I do not believe that Wittgenstein envisions a static assemblage of individuals neurologically capable of meaningful engagement with objects in their proximate environment. Rather, he has in mind individuals with—if I may paraphrase him as speaking anachronistically in our contemporary "language of the natural sciences"—homologous *plus* generalized neurological structures *plus* hormonal effects, and so on, *who are not merely innately capable of socialization, but are indeed socially engaged.* This means that our neurology cannot be imaged and mapped—in other words, cannot be *interpreted*—in isolation from the background. Someone may object at this point that I am begging the question regarding affective intentionality by conflating the necessary intentionality of our language (language always *intends*) with the alleged intentionality of our mental dispositions. This is not the case. Rather, I am offering the settled scientific observation that the necessary conditions for language acquisition include both what Wexel referred to above as the "plasticity" of our neurological architecture *and* the shaping of that structure by virtue of the subject's embodiment in our social form of life.

Wittgenstein continues, "If language is to be a means of communication there must be agreement not only in definitions but also (queer as this may sound) in judgments (*eine Übereinstimmung in den Urteil*)."[71] Such judgments are not made within the privacy of one's brain, but in the public space where our lives are lived together. In a previous paragraph, this agreement is described as agreement in *Lebensform*.[72] This judgment or agreement in form of life indicates that our inner feelings are not inner, private sensations after all. They are what they are out there, in our shared social space. Apart from our cognizing, beyond our willing, our feelings are what they are in our social context. They are, contra Luntley's worry over the unstructured character of such given items, a nonvolitional and noncognitive aspect of our human constitution.[73] We are constituted by our neurological capacities, yes, but also by more than our interior neurological capacities; we are essentially social beings, much as Aristotle the empiricist maintained over two millennia ago.

71. Wittgenstein, *Philosophical Investigations*, paragraph 242.

72. Ibid., paragraph 241.

73. Professor Tallon refers to volition, cognition, and affect (to which category I relate *Angst*) as the "irreducible intentionalities" of our triune consciousness. See Tallon, *Head and Heart*, 3–4.

Our constitution is not mere thingly existence or *Sein*; instead, we are *Dasein*, socially and thus spatiotemporally situated beings. On this basis a validation or calibration is possible between our world and our selves, that is, on the basis of our feelings, such as our feeling pain (Wittgenstein's premier analytic example), our feeling *Angst* (Heidegger's celebrated affect), or our feeling joy (Wittgenstein's preferred mood). The social world "supports the focus of individual attitudes" or feelings; it "scaffolds the engagement of the will with that which is independent of the will. Similar thoughts apply to 'form of life.'"[74] So, then, is this a piece of a last-generation continental, phenomenological argument or a contribution to the social neuroscience of emotional intentionality? It is a contribution to a wider neuroscience of emotion.

In a manner similar to the way we "find ourselves" in the earth's electromagnetic field (a location that can be verified by the use of a compass), in our moods we find ourselves already in the world in an unmediated way (this is Heidegger's *Befindlichkeit*). While the structure of this ongoing, intentional engagement is something that we can discern, it is not something that we can readily alter, cognitively and willfully. This inability of one intentionality to grasp or "manhandle" another is one of the clearest and most experiential proofs of their mutual irreducibilities. Beyond this, *the intentional engagement with the world as a whole that we feel in a given mood is also a conduit by which the world shapes our neurology*. This is a substantial contribution of social neuroscience to our understanding of what it means to be in the world emotionally.

Although the newly emerging discipline of social neuroscience has only begun to research the two-way bridge between our neurology and our social existence, its promise for the empirical or third-person verification (and thus a suitable twenty-first century phenomenological validation) of the intentionality of moods is latent in its already-documented research into facial recognition. According to findings very recently published by Wexler,[75] Levinas' argument for the ethical and ontological primacy of face-to-face interaction, based upon Heidegger's discovery of the intentionality of moods, has a neurology that is best understood as a neurology *shaped by* our social interaction. There is a neurological plasticity observable in the orbitofrontal cortices and the amygdala of individuals engaged in face-to-face interactions with one

74. Luntley, *Wittgenstein*, 145.
75. Wexler, *Brain and Culture*, 33–36.

another. While wanting to avoid the charge of anachronistic analogizing, I will say that Wittgenstein and Heidegger (as well, of course, as Levinas) may be read as pointing the way to such a socially grounded neuroscience of our moods. Nowhere is this clearer than in the many volumes Paul Eckman has devoted to facial recognition, research that Brothers has cited with approval as the basis for her claim that we are "hardwired" for the social.[76] This is not to say that the "hardwiring" spontaneously produces society, of course, but that the neurology-to-world fit is as well a world-to-neurology fit. This fitness or attunement comes out in our judgments, which themselves presuppose our conscious and emotional experience of being-in-the-world. The expression of our judgments is cognitive, but what these judgments are judging is the propriety, the character, or whatever, of the already-existent mood. Wittgenstein has more on the matter of judgment.

In the less familiar second part of *Philosophical Investigations,* Wittgenstein explains that the genuineness of our expressions of feelings depend, not upon properly warranted epistemological claims, but upon expert judgments by persons with substantial experience in being human beings (already engaged in what Heidegger would call "being-in-the-world" but which Wittgenstein describes as the activity of *Lebensform*).

> Is there such a thing as "expert judgment" about the genuineness of expressions of feeling?—Even here, there are those whose judgment is "better" and whose judgment is "worse." Correcter prognoses will generally issue from the judgments of those with better knowledge of mankind. Can one learn this knowledge? Yes; some can. Not, however, by taking a course in it, but through "*experience.*"—Can someone else be a man's teacher in this? Certainly. From time to time he gives him the right tip.—This is what "learning" and "teaching" are like here.—What one acquires here is not a technique; one learns correct judgments. There are also rules, but they do not form a system, and only experienced people can apply them right. Unlike calculating rules. What is most difficult here is to put this indefiniteness, correctly and unfalsified, into words.[77]

---

76. For a select list of Ekman's work on body and facial movement, see Brothers, *Friday's Footprint*, 166.

77. Wittgenstein, *Philosophical Investigations*, 227e.

Who are those people with such a "better knowledge of mankind"? Think of those modern authors who do not place everything in our subjective experience under the category of the cognitive, but elucidate as well our emotional experience as human beings. These authors include existential philosophers such as Heidegger and Kierkegaard as well as poets such as Hopkins, Rilke, Hölderlin, and perhaps the Wittgenstein scholar and poet John Koethe. We might think as well of scientific experts (Wittgenstein was not a linguist, but a philosopher of mathematics) with *a sufficiently broad field of reference* to identify a feeling in respect to the performances of its inner-outer, neurological, and social components, as well as to account for their dynamic interrelatedness.

By "the genuineness of expressions of a feeling," then, does Wittgenstein mean, for example, of a smile as a bona fide expression of happiness versus a social smile (as one might undertake to demonstrate in an isolated and controlled psychological study), or is he referring as well to the authenticity of the feeling being expressed by an I-Thou transaction within our shared world? Inasmuch as we have heard him explain that "other people cannot be said to learn of my sensations *only* from my behavior,"[78] we may see in the seasoned judgment of those with experience an acquaintance with the feeling that they have themselves validated over their lifetime and that they recognize as well in the situation of others. This ongoing interaction enables us to adjust our analyses, inclusive of our neurological understandings, but not exclusive of the background, of our emotional feelings in all their complex interrelatedness.

There is no hint of Cartesian materialism here in which everything is reduced to the cogitation within the subject's head. Instead, Wittgenstein's commentary on the genuineness of expressions of intentional feelings in the course of our *Lebensform* proceeds on the basis of simple subjectivism in which the full range of a subject's performances are taken, as a matter of course, to be what we all have as human persons *in the world*. These experts are themselves proceeding to make their judgments of authenticity on the basis of their own experience of our common felt openness, as Heidegger would say, to the being of other human beings *In-der-Welt-Sein*.

But how precisely is this scientifically approachable? Wittgenstein alludes to this fundamental openness as an *ineffable* background: "Perhaps what is inexpressible (what I find mysterious and am not able

---

78. Ibid., paragraph 246.

to express) is the background (*den Hintergrund*) against which whatever I could express has its meaning."[79] I will take this to mean that the background was *scientifically* ineffable in Wittgenstein's day. His analysis is suggestive of the need for a fuller science, a neuroscience or a *social affective neuroscience* such as cited earlier in the work of Rockwell, Brothers, and Wexler. This background is Wittgenstein's ground or what I have called the quasi-intentional formal object of the world as a whole, the felt sense of engagement with the world such as we experience it in our *Angst*. The background, then, is the ground of our emotional intentionality. This suggests that a consideration of social constructivism in connection with neuroscientific research concerning affective intentionality would be in order. We move next to an objection to my case for a suitable social neuroscientific study of *Angst* and its affective intentionality by John Searle. Searle's objection to the sort of field theory I see in Wittgenstein's concept of the background is, ironically, based on a reading of Wittgenstein's concept of the background.

AN OBJECTION FROM SEARLE

Might social constructivism collaborate with social neuroscience in the locating of moods and their intentionality within the behavioral field? Let us next consider Searle's social constructivism and the challenge it poses for my argument.[80] After having elaborated how Wittgenstein, in sympathy with Heidegger, might consider an individual's *Angst* in terms of *Lebensform* as an (noncognitive but not irrational) indexing of oneself in relation to one's world, it will be helpful to note that, despite the social constructivist interpretation of it promoted by Searle,[81] Wittgenstein's concept of the background is more robustly social than is typically acknowledged.[82]

As we have seen, Wittgenstein says that there is an ineffable background against which anything expressible has its meaning.[83] We can take this as meaning that the background is ineffable in the sense of

---

79. Wittgenstein, *Culture and Value*, 16e.

80. Searle, *The Construction of Social Reality*, esp. "Background Abilities and the Explanation of Social Phenomena," 127–48.

81. See Barbiero, "The Background."

82. For a related consideration of Wittgenstein's social constructivism at the institutional level, see my "David Bloor," 37–38.

83. Wittgenstein, *Culture and Value*, 16e, quoted supra.

being beyond words but not beyond all consciousness. There is an additional option. The background, I will say at this juncture, is not beyond *affect*. In another place, Wittgenstein writes that it is on the basis or condition of this background that we determine our judgments, concepts, and actions.[84] As a ground, this background provides a normative "place and time" within which we can validate, calibrate, or "discover the truth of" our feeling of *Angst* as something meaningful (that is, of the world) not of our own creation. There is, in our social transactions, a public recognition. That is to say, we regularly judge both the genuineness of the subjective feeling as such and the appropriate expressive interactions regarding that feeling, such as our attunement in *Angst* toward everything on the whole. In our moods, we already find ourselves disposed before we know it; in our social intercourse, we further "test fly" the fit of these feelings.

So, we can and do judge for ourselves and in community with others whether our mood of anguish is an appropriate stance toward the world in which we live. Examples of this would be the argument against an automatic therapeutic remedy to anguish such as Peter Kramer's in *Listening to Prozac*,[85] or the counsel not to be anxious about anything offered by Paul in his New Testament epistle to the Philippians. Within our active *Lebensform*, we can judge rightly, we could say, given a substantial amount of experience over time. Our linguistic signs function normatively on the basis of our engagement with this background. Our use of language, with its inherent aptness for discriminating between right ways and wrong ways to judge expressions of our feelings and emotions, thus validates the genuineness of various expressions of feelings on the basis of what is *shown* to be the case in our everyday form of life and is thereby *known* to be the case.[86]

---

84. Wittgenstein, *Remarks on the Philosophy of Psychology*.

85. Kramer, *Listening to Prozac*: "Anxiety is at the heart of the psychological understanding of man. The 'dynamic' in psychodynamic psychotherapy is anxiety; anxiety is the motor force behind psychoanalysis . . . Beyond the profession, in the work of existential prophets like Kierkegaard and Heidegger, the individual's struggle with anxiety is the preferred route to self-discovery," xii. Kramer argues against the uncritical pharmacological use of "mood brighteners" such as Prozac.

86. According to St. Ignatius' *Spiritual Exercises*, "discernment of spirits" in the third way is presented as the best sign of the individual's "state of soul." This is from Andrew Tallon in personal correspondence (9/19/06).

All of this recommends a shift in our scientific thinking to an extensional concept of "mind" and as well into a recognition that our neurology is twice-embodied. Whereas we are in the habit of locating anxiety within the mind of the (perhaps pathological) individual, it would be more apropos to locate this mood in-the-world. In terms borrowed from twentieth-century physics, this means construing moods and their intentionality not in terms of (Newtonian) substantial subjects who somehow exert a power over the other objects within the range of their powers, but rather in terms of field theory. Moods are not narrowly subjective powers, as if our moods, like the active sonar of a submerged submarine, serve as echo-locators of nearby objects; instead, moods are the currents of the ocean in which we swim. Moods are part and parcel of our existence as human subjects embodied in a wide, wide world. Now, how does contemporary social constructivist emotional theory benefit from an understanding of this Wittgensteinian background? The answer lies in the constructivist's misunderstanding of the place of intentionality.

We could look, for example, to John Searle's notion of what he identifies as "the Background." You may recall that I have already mentioned in my first chapter how Searle embraces intentionality but specifically discounts the intentionality of what he calls "forms of undirected anxiety."[87] In his later writings, Searle articulates more of his view of the intentionality of moods. This leads me to his more recent writings regarding the Background. "In my writings on issues in the philosophy of mind and the philosophy of language," Searle explains, "I have argued for what I call the thesis of the Background: Intentional states function only given a set of Background capacities that do not themselves consist in intentional phenomena."[88] At first reading, it may seem that Searle has been writing on these issues from a Wittgensteinian perspective, such as I have just proposed. But this is not, in my view, a reading of Wittgenstein that is supported by Wittgenstein's own texts. In defining his term "capacities" Searle says, "By *capacities* I mean abilities, dispositions, tendencies, and *causal structures generally*."[89] We may begin to wonder where these causal structures are located, but to this point his thesis appears to accord with Wittgenstein's *Investigations* and

---

87. Searle, *Intentionality*, 1–36, esp. 1.
88. Searle, *The Construction of Social Reality*, 129.
89. Ibid.

perhaps to include a gesture toward *Tractatus* as well. He appears to be on the way to articulating a position very similar to mine that *Angst* is intentional. But what does he mean by "causal structures"? By "causal structures" Searle means our intercranial neurology. Furthermore, the direction of causation is centripetal, from brain to society.

Searle's notion of background is, at its foundation, predominately inner biology, making his theory of intentionality decidedly centripetal, as I have mentioned, and somewhat negligent as a consequence of the individual's engagement in *Lebensform* as taught us in Wittgenstein's *Investigations*. For Searle, the causal structures that account for intentionality are internal structures, themselves by themselves, although their capacities manifest themselves on a larger, societal scale. "It is important to see that when we talk about the Background we are talking about a certain category of neurophysiological causation."[90] Note his claim of "neurophysiological *causation*." He is at pains to preempt the very objection to Cartesian materialism that we have been reading in Wittgenstein himself, namely, that the analysis of a feeling cannot be conducted below the level of the socially engaged subject.

Searle continues by mentioning that there is "nothing disreputable" in equating neurophysiological causation with what Wittgenstein insists is a linguistic background inasmuch as "because we do not know how these structures function at a neurophysiological level, we are forced to describe them at a much higher level. . . . When I say, for example, that I am able to speak English, I am talking about a causal capacity of my brain . . ."[91] But are we (or is Wittgenstein) forced away from our linguistic practices altogether in favor of an overwhelmingly neurophysiological explanation? Might it not rather be the case that we require a suitably complex, interactive grasp of the neurobiological-social interplay of, for instance, our higher emotions and the moods of joy and *Angst* in order to conduct our neurological research? In a word, instead of subsuming our social world under our biology, why not acknowledge that the subject interacting with her environment, especially her social environment, is the natural supervenience base of intentionality, including emotional intentionality?

As mentioned when beginning my consideration of Searle's constructivist objection to my intentionality thesis, there is a problem in

90. Ibid.
91. Ibid.

where he locates intentionality. In a nutshell, he does not see intentionality as an intrinsic feature of our world, whereas I do. The difficulty with Searle's intentionality thesis as it is carried out in his discussion of the background is due to what Rockwell identifies as "Searle's Intrinsicality Argument."[92] "The intrinsicality argument claims that physical characteristics are somehow intrinsic to things, but intentional characteristics are not."[93] This means that, for Searle, physical reality is absolute, whereas intentionality is epiphenomenal. This assumption leads Searle to postulate that, if all observers were to be deleted from the world, the features that we identify as "mass," "gravitational attraction," and "molecule" would remain unaffected, whereas "bathtubs" and "chairs" would cease to be features of the world. This is so, Searle contends, because mass, gravitation, and molecules are intrinsic features of the world, whereas bathtubs and chairs are features that are relative to the observers of the world.[94] At the heart of this distinction between intrinsic features and relative features, as Rockwell explains, is a conflation of relative features with assigned features. Suppose we grant that, absent the people who sit in them, chairs cannot be chairs. It is also true that, absent the circulatory systems of which they are a part, hearts cannot be hearts. Absent the system or field of which they are part, neurons cannot be neurons.

This leads to one reply to Searle's intrinsicality argument: "Certain entities are constituted by relationships that do not obviously refer to or presuppose the existence of human beings. But even such entities as the chemical elements presuppose certain relationships . . ."[95] For instance, the chemical elements presuppose certain relationships to scientific procedures and metrics. As Rockwell points out, it would be positively incoherent for someone to maintain that a given substance is sulfur, even if it does not behave as the element identified by block sixteen on the periodic table would behave in the lab.

According to Rockwell, there is a stronger response to Searle's argument that physical characteristics are somehow intrinsic, whereas intentional characteristics are not. This stronger claim is "that the relational characteristics that define things in terms of biological functions,

---

92. Rockwell, *Neither Brain Nor Ghost*, 141–46. The following is my summary of Rockwell, inclusive of his analysis of the earlier Searle on this point.

93. Ibid., 141.

94. Searle, *The Rediscovery of the Mind*, 211.

95. Rockwell, *Neither Brain Nor Ghost*, 143.

or human goals and values, are every bit as real as the characteristics described by physics."[96] To put this in another way, I would say that Searle, for all his familiarity with the Wittgenstein of the *Investigations*, has not extricated himself completely from the logical atomism of the *Tractatus*. Searle oscillates between logical atomism and a more dynamic system understanding of intentionality. As a case in point, at the same time that he is pushing his intrinsicality argument, he observes that "in order to have one belief or desire, I have to have a whole network of other beliefs and desires."[97] As Rockwell indicates, this ought to lead Searle to reject the existence of intrinsic properties since if at least some of our assessments of the world are correct, there must be a relationship, an "inter-fact" relationship, in order to validate any single fact. No standalone fact can be a fact. Rockwell concludes that we ought, accordingly, to dismiss Searle's distinction between the observer-relative and the intrinsic, or between institutional facts and brute facts.[98] This means, in my view, that the brute facts of our biology or the intrinsic properties of our neurology are as much part and parcel of the field of consciousness as are affective intentionalities, and vice versa. From this it follows that, just as intentionality ought not to be reduced to its neurobiological aspect, neither ought the neurobiology of a mood's intentionality be researched apart from our *Umwelt*, the world brought into view (or, if you prefer, the background brought to the foreground) by the mood's intentionality.

So then, Searle's argument runs this way: in order to give us a feel for how the social Background, which is independent of the "intentional contents" of our minds, works, we must acknowledge that the Background, that is, social reality as something separate and apart from, but nevertheless parasitic upon, the intentional contents of one's mind, which is what enables linguistic interpretation to take place. But why speak of the intentional contents of one's mind as if intentionality subsists completely within the brain? Searle's Background enables perceptual interpretation to take place and, in fact, the percepts thus structure consciousness. Temporally extended sequences of experiences come to us with a narrative or dramatic shape as "dramatic categories" and each of us has "a set of motivational dispositions" that condition the structure of our experience. In addition, the Background facilitates "certain kinds

96. Ibid.
97. Searle, *The Rediscovery of the Mind*, 176.
98. Rockwell, *Neither Brain Nor Ghost*, 145.

of readiness" and "disposes me to certain sorts of behavior." We have already reckoned with Searle's presupposition of intrinsic properties of a certain sort, in combination with his conflation of relative features and assigned features. On this basis, I believe we can debunk Searle's dismissal of the intentionality of moods such as *Angst* or "diffuse anxiety."

It is also possible, in light of comments in subsequent writings, to see this as one instance of "nothing-but" theorizing that slipped by Professor Searle. There is, it may seem at first, no reason why he could not allow for the intentionality of diffuse anxiety if he were to consider the quasi- or nonobjective intentionality such as I have elaborated.[99] Indeed, he seems to come very close to allowing this when, in his discussion of "Consciousness and Its Structure," he insists that "all of our conscious states come to us in one *mood* or another. We are always in some mood . . . there is what one might call a certain flavor to my experiences. This flavor is what I mean by mood. Any conscious state you may have always comes with some sort of coloration."[100] However, the mere mention of moods as "coloration" shows that Searle is decidedly not interested in acknowledging the intentionality of noncognitive emotions. Mood in this sense of "flavor" is paradigmatically nonintentional. Moods remain, for Searle, first-person *qualia* and nothing more.

Wittgenstein himself, unlike Searle's Wittgenstein, leaves the door open for emotional intentionality. Furthermore, he leaves the door open for the quasi-intentionality of *Angst*, a mood that intends the world as a whole. Consider his analysis of joy. "But I do have a real *feeling* of joy! . . . but of course joy is not joyful behavior, nor yet a feeling round the corners of the mouth and eyes."[101] This is another way of saying that joy is what Heidegger would analyze as "primordial," a decidedly non-behaviorist understanding of this feeling. Wittgenstein continues by articulating the position of an imagined interlocutor. "'But "joy" surely designates an inward thing.' No. 'Joy' designates nothing at all. Neither any inward nor any outward thing."[102] To this I will add the gloss that joy is intentional, embracing both the self (there is a neurological aspect) and the world (this is its formal object). In this sense it is "neither

---

99. For a complementary treatment of intentionality in Wittgenstein, see Thornton, *Wittgenstein on Language and Thought*, 2.

100. Searle, *Mind, Language, and Society*, 77.

101. Anscombe and von Wright, *Ludwig Wittgenstein*, paragraph 487, see also 486.

102. Ibid.

any (exclusively) inward nor any (exclusively) outward *thing*." Heidegger the continental thinker describes how our feeling brings "perdurance" or an enduring engagement with the world. Wittgenstein the analytic philosopher fends off less-than-rigorous thinking that seeks to deny or denigrate the enduring character of our more-than-cognitive relationships in and with the world.

I will not say that Wittgenstein is as concerned as Heidegger is to unpack our being in time. Nevertheless, Wittgenstein is alert to the temporality of the individual who is in the mood of joy temporally. He considers that his interlocutor could say, "But you talk as if I weren't really expecting, hoping, *now*—as I thought I was. As if what were happening *now* had no deep significance."[103] To this, Wittgenstein responds, first, by challenging the notion that what happens to be present *now* has value over and against the long-term experience of the subject: "What does it mean to say 'What is happening now has significance' or 'has deep significance'?"[104] This response is congruent with the notion of a mood's long-term intentionality toward the background. Second, he sets the discussion back on the firm ground of the subject's lifelong social or situated experience. "What is a *deep* feeling? Could someone have a feeling of ardent love or hope for the space of one second—*no matter what* preceded or followed this second?—What is happening now has significance—in these surroundings."[105] What are these surroundings or *Umgebung*? The surroundings are our *human* life in the world as we indeed live it. "The surroundings give [what is happening in feeling hope etc.] its significance. And the word 'hope' refers to a phenomenon of human life (*menschlichen Lebens*)."[106] The surroundings are our *Lebensform* (Wittgenstein) in which we come to know ourselves as *Dasein* (Heidegger) on the basis of our felt situatedness. Intentionality is thus secured as an irreducible feature of our feeling being.

What are the consequences for emotional theory and then for our understanding of feelings such as joy or *Angst* for Wittgenstein's skepticism regarding the philosophical value of seeking "nothing but" theories of deeper, inner content in order to establish the scientific worth of our feelings such as joy? Wittgenstein obliges us to return again and again

---

103. Wittgenstein, *Philosophical Investigations*, paragraph 583.
104. Ibid.
105. Ibid.
106. Ibid.

from the introspective worlds created by reductive emotional theories to our pre-philosophical everyday experience—to our common human space-time, the common sense world where we experience the regular validation of emotional states and of feelings such as *Angst*. An obsessive retreat into the self, any attempt to depend exclusively upon, say, Cartesian *cogito* or Hobbesian mechanisms for a theory of emotion, is cut off at the pass by the pre-theoretical publicity of *Lebensform*, language, and discourse. Our feelings are known within the field of our form of life. This is true of our feelings of joy, of hope, and of *Angst*. Further, we can envision a natural-science treatment of our emotions and moods, as I have mentioned, in social neuroscience.

Leslie Brothers, a research neuroscientist, writes, for example, of the interesting promise provided to the practice of social neuroscience by the use of technologies such as human functional magnetic resonance imaging (fMRI) for understanding what is happening in two realms of our social interactivities, recognizing how we experience face-to-face interactions as well as what is going on when we respond selectively to the voices of other persons.[107] According to fMRI experimentation as reported beginning in 1995, an area of the ventral posterior lobes adjoining the occipital lobes is specifically activated by the sight of faces. This discovery has led one researcher to label the fusiform gyrus, a patch of cortex on the bottom surface of the brain, "the fusiform face area." Related studies of the fusiform gyrus involving the plotting of electrical potentials has demonstrated that space-specific brain activity involves as well the neighboring inferior temporal gyrus and occipitotemporal sulcus.

Although results in this area are less definitive, it appears that certain areas of the brain are dedicated as well to auditory recognition. A report published in 2000 documents how, by means of fMRI imaging, a region of cortex on the upper bank of the central superior temporal sulcus has been shown to respond selectively to voice stimuli as distinct from other types of sounds.

Again according to Brothers, positron emission tomography (PET scans) conducted in 1996 indicates the possibility of identifying, in terms of metabolic brain activity, a system for producing and interpreting

---

107. See "Social Neuroscience" in Brothers, *Friday's Footprint*, 79–86. The following paragraphs are a collation of these select contributions to social neuroscience as provided by Brothers.

goal-directed actions in intra-personal space.[108] This is germane to my consideration of a mood's intentionality because "goal-directed actions" is the neurological, operational definition of intentionality. "Expressions of body, face, and voice, and the direction of gaze, when combined, are the building blocks of what we call 'intentions.'"[109]

Furthermore, the evidence of the electrical stimulation of the amygdala and hippocampus of a patient prone to seizures the neurologist Pierre Gloor discovered that he was evoking feelings that could only be described by his patient as social feelings.

According to Brothers, what struck Gloor was the social character of the patient's descriptions of his (electrically evoked) feelings. They were descriptions of feelings such as we have only as the result of someone else's disposition toward us. The identity of the "someone" was vague: "Upon stimulating his left amygdale at 1 mA, he had a feeling 'as if I were not belonging here,' which he likened to being at a party and not being welcome. . . . Right hippocampal stimulation at 3 mA induced anxiety and guilt, '. . .like you are demanding to hand in a report that was due 2 weeks ago . . . as if I were guilty of some form of tardiness.'"[110] So, not only does such clinical research verify the reality of our own (outward-reaching) intentions, but our comprehension of the intentions of others toward us as well. As reported by Brothers, "The far reaches of what we understand about the brain and social cognition is a recent discovery regarding the understanding of social exchange."[111] A patient with bilateral damage to his orbitofrontal cortex and anterior temporal cortex, while able to handle cognitive tasks such as applying rules of workplace safety was nevertheless significantly impaired when it came to tasks that involved social contract reasoning, such as involve an appreciation of our responsibilities toward one another. The author notes that this is very preliminary, but may be suggestive of discrete brain functions for the rational applications of rules of behavior toward impersonal situations on the one hand and intrapersonal situations on the other.

108. Brothers, *Friday's Footprint*, 81

109. Ibid., 82

110. Gloor, "The Role of the Human Limbic System," 159–69. Cited in Brothers, *Friday's Footprint*, 82–83.

111. Brothers, *Friday's Footprint*, 85. See as well 85–86 and Stone, "Selective Impairment of Social Inferences Following Orbitofrontal Cortex Damage."

SUMMARY

In summary, emotional feelings and in particular higher-level or higher cognitive emotions are intentional and thus objective engagements with the world. This is a fortiori the case with moods. In terms more familiar to analytic thinkers, emotional feelings that have the character of moods have what Wittgenstein calls the *background* or the whole hurly-burly of our human form of life as their field of validation. But this is not to be understood in the sense that Searle has given to his concept of the Background, in which relative features of reality are conflated with assigned features as if only physical properties were intrinsic whereas intentional characteristics are not. Intentional characteristics are objective, according to social neuroscience. Thus, moods and their intentionality have a social and neuroscientific grounding that is amenable to study by the emerging science of social neuroscience.

And so, with an eye on the promise that *social* neuroscience holds for the scientific verification—and thereby for the philosophical validation—of a mood, let me recapitulate the significance of a mood such as *Angst* for human beings. Affects position us in this world. Basic emotions, that is, emotions such as fear and anger, which we human beings have in common with lower animals, are evidence of our immediate engagement with the world. This engagement is, for the most part, a matter of autonomic affect programs. Higher cognitive emotions such as rage evince our immediate engagement with the world in a more long-term and more evaluative manner. Higher emotions entail reflection and a degree of cognition over and above basic emotions. Nor is this an argument for emotional intentionality as if *Angst* were a (mere) *quale*, possessing only a first-person narrative "ontology" of some sort. On the contrary, a mood such as this has ontic or factual reality and is thus available for scientific, third-person testing, or verification as to its role in human beings and their form of life.

We ought, then, to be able to establish objectively the physical substrata of intentionality in a way that explains how it does what it does. I have identified our affective intentionality as "twice-embodied," meaning by this that "the supervenience base for all mental events, including subjective experiences, includes not only brain events, but events in the rest of the body and in those parts of the environment with which

How the Mood of Angst Might Be Verified Empirically

the conscious organism maintains a synergetic relationship."[112] It seems reasonable to expect that social neuroscience, as it develops into a more long-term study of the human brain in the context of human society, may well document evidence of the long-term effects of specific moods in the evolution of the human brain attuned to the world we care about.

By way of brief excursus, it may be the case that the social neuroscientific study of autism will deliver further support for my thesis. As Panksepp notes, "The existence of this syndrome affords investigators a unique opportunity to study the workings of social emotional systems in human beings."[113] Understandably, Panksepp speaks of the workings of these systems *in* human beings. At this point in the development of my thesis, I would prefer to paraphrase him in such a way as to emphasize the need to include the social field in this investigation. Investigations into autism afford a unique opportunity, I would say, to study the workings of social and emotional systems *within and among* human beings. For example, on the basis of the kind of validation of affective intentionality such as I am proposing, it seems plausible that in the case of the relationship between an autistic child and his mother, just as the gross brain and fine structural or neuronal abnormalities contribute to deficits in communication, socialization, and imagination, so too the mother's devoted interaction with her child will have an effect on the neurology of her child. This is to be expected because of the reality of the emotional field, which includes not only the child's neurology but also the child's interaction with his mother.

Basic emotions do not require much of a field theory. However, moods such as *Angst* or joy[114] do—that is, they are not reducible to inner cognitions, but are rather felt, nonmediated engagements *with the world*. Moods do not simply endure; rather, as Heidegger puts it, moods "bring perdurance" to our lives as being in the world. Moods are the climate of our human being in the world in the sense of the world as "what we care about." We cannot know a world that we do not care about. From the fact that "emotion is an inter-individual process that alters the momentary

---

112. Rockwell, *Neither Brain Nor Ghost*, 206.

113. Panksepp, *Affective Neuroscience*. See especially "Additional Psychiatric Implications: Autism and Brain Socioemotional Systems," 276–78.

114. Although my concern has been with *Angst*, the "most celebrated continental mood" (Tallon) other moods would be, for example, joy and equanimity. For Heidegger's palette of moods see Smith, "On Heidegger's Theory of Moods."

functional organization of the brains of the interactants, configuring and activating certain multiunit functional systems and dismantling and deactivating others,"[115] it follows that a mood can be validated as it is objectively verifiable on the basis of long-term alterations of the functional organizations of the brains of the interacting individuals as calibrated within a social environment. A mood's objectivity is thus verified in an objective, third-person manner by its intentionality within what we may call a dynamic system, the context of our living, spatio-temporal engagement with the world. So, then, the mood at the center of the present study, *Angst*, pre-cognitively and pre-volitionally reveals the nature of human being as in-the-world in its full ontological and social meaning.

AFTERTHOUGHT:[116]
... ET INQUIETUM EST COR NOSTRUM ...

At the conclusion of this argument for the study of affective intentionality in the emerging discipline of social neuroscience, it would seem plausible to construe *Angst* as a normative datum whereby a human being can know herself as more than a cognitive and willful being on the basis of her regular engagement within our *Lebensform* in an emotional and intentional manner. In the familiar phenomenological and existential idiom of the last century, we would speak of "being authentic." This brings us back to what Heidegger says of *Angst* in his existential analysis of conscience, making *Angst* the ground for our potential to be responsible selves. By being attentive to our feeling *Angst*, we have something to think about, something to cognize *regarding our selves already engaged with our world*, but as to which direction this cognition will next lead is not determined by our feeling *Angst*.

"Authenticity" in the vocabulary of a continental philosopher such as Heidegger entails (1) a serious view of life as a necessary condition, but involves, in addition, (2) conscious attention to conscience. On Heidegger's existential analysis of conscience, it is what I have identified as our irrefragable feeling of *Angst* that must give us pause.[117] In this

---

115. Wexler, *Brain and Culture*, 34.

116. See Panksepp, *Affective Neuroscience*, 6–7. Panksepp explains, "'Afterthought' ... is used to give focused attention to key issues, especially historic or conceptual ones, that do not fit well in the main text. Indeed, the 'Afterthoughts' will often highlight the most critical issues ..."

117. See Heidegger, *Being and Time*, 247–77, esp., e.g., 255: "Uncanniness reveals itself authentically in the fundamental attunement of *Angst*, and, as the most elemental

respect, *Angst* as a mood is quite distinct from the moods of equanimity or joy.

When we are inoculated against "nothing but" biological explanations and psychological descriptions of *Angst*, the rich phenomenon of *Angst* is disclosed as socially valid. That is, as a feeling it is irrefragable, an experience *in* consciousness but pointing *beyond* consciousness. Its meaning is given, as Buber might say, in the "between." This feeling is thus self-authenticating, but it is not self-interpreting. As Heidegger has it, "The call [that is, the elemental *Angst*-call of conscience] does not report any facts; it calls without uttering anything. The call speaks in the uncanny mode of *silence*."[118] This means that *Angst* is a prime datum for our thinking and cognition about ourselves as human beings. Now, this prime datum of human being can be cognitively construed in two ways. One way to appreciate the impact of these two interpretations is to ask, "Is our feeling of *Angst* epilogue or prologue for what we can now understand of ourselves, engaged as we are with our world?"[119]

We may think that our feeling of *Angst* is an epilogue. In other words, from the potential to be a self, which we realize when we are cognizant of our feeling of *Angst*, we may proceed to what I shall call a nonreligious resolution. In the concluding sentences of *Being and Nothingness*, Jean-Paul Sartre asserts, "Every human reality is a passion in that it projects losing itself so as to found being ... Thus the passion of man is the reverse of that of Christ, for man loses himself as a man in order that God may be born. But the idea of God is contradictory and we lose ourselves in vain. Man is a useless passion."[120] And yet, it would seem that this cannot be the last word on our feelings. If man is "a useless passion" we are entitled to acknowledge, strictly speaking, not that

---

disclosedness of thrown Da-sein, it confronts being-in-the-world with the nothingness of the world about which it is anxious in the *Angst* about its inmost potentiality-of-being revealed in *Angst*. What if Da-sein, finding itself in the ground of its uncanniness, were the caller of the call of conscience?"

118. Ibid., 255.

119. This question was suggested in Schacht, *Making Sense of Nietzsche*, 39. Professor Schacht is not discussing *Angst*, but the ambiguity of Nietzsche's concept of nihilism when he writes, "Given that Nietzsche holds a period of nihilism to be inevitable following the collapse of the 'Christian-moral' interpretation of the world, the question arises of his attitude toward it. The answer to this question is two-fold, because his attitude toward it depends on whether it has the character of epilogue or prologue."

120. Sartre, *Being and Nothingness*, 615.

our feelings are useless, but that we have failed to discover any value to our passions *cognitively*. This conclusion is not a feeling but a cognitive conclusion about a feeling.

As I recently heard Robert Solomon put it in his lecture on the intelligence of emotions, "Sartre picks up from Husserl and Heidegger the idea of emotions as a way of being in the world, and gives it a unique twist. What he wants to say is that what they have shown is that emotions are not simply objects in the world that we somehow experience in an odd way, but emotions are rather our own actions."[121] Seen in this way, *Angst* is, I will say, an epilogue. It is interpreted to be a dead end in the sense that it is not revelatory of our kind of being but is the end of self-discovery. One could, as I have said, regard this as a nonreligious interpretation of this mood.

Alternatively, given that there is an *extra nos* or not-of-our-own-doing character to *Angst*, such as is being verified in the social neuroscience cited by Brothers and Rockwell, we may well see our feeling of *Angst* as a prologue. That is, we can, in step with Heidegger, begin with the realization that *Angst* assails us and thus from the potential to be a self, which we realize when we are cognizant of our feeling *Angst*, we may proceed to a religious resolution. The classic example of such a religious resolution of *Angst* is found in the opening paragraph of Augustine's *Confessions*: *Quia fecisti nos ad te et inquietum est cor nostrum, donec requiescat in te*.[122] "... You [that is, the Lord God] have made us for Yourself and our heart is disquieted until it finds itself quieted in You." I shall paraphrase Augustine as praying to God, "Our heart is *Angst*-ridden and *unheimlich* unless and until we find ourselves at home in You."

Heidegger in fact provides what we may construe as a pre-religious view of *Angst* as prologue. That is to say, he regards our feeling of *Angst* as disclosive of our potential for being responsible selves, but insofar as *Angst* as a feeling in the phenomenon of conscience "does not report any facts,"[123] where we go from the feeling to the interpretation of the feeling, for our form of life remains an open question intellectually.

Now there is a direction in which Heidegger wants to lead our thinking here. This direction is toward the inevitable approach of our own death, which he famously denotes as our "being-toward-death," but

---

121. Solomon, "Are Emotions 'in' the Mind?"
122. Augustine, *Confessions*, 2.
123. Heidegger, *Being and Time*, 255.

which is described in his analysis of conscience as "that of which *Angst* 'is anxious.'"[124] The more familiar locution, "being-toward-death" is a feature of his analysis of *Dasein*, which, you will recall from my treatment of his existential analysis of conscience in the opening chapter, he hypothesizes to be both the called and caller in the phenomenon of conscience. He writes of "the fundamental attunement of *Angst*" that "as the most elemental disclosedness of thrown Da-sein," in fact *Dasein* "confronts being-in-the-world with the nothingness of the world about which it is anxious in the *Angst* about its inmost potentiality-of-being revealed in *Angst*." Then follows his hypothesis: "*What if Da-sein, finding itself in the ground of its uncanniness, were the caller of the call of conscience?*"[125]

But to the reader of *Being and Time*, the silent call of *Angst* is purely an unavoidable feeling of disquiet, homelessness, unsettledness. It does not identify itself as a call or a potential. The call, the notion of conscience, a knowing in connection with, is supplied in the cognitive, evaluative process that goes to work on the phenomenon of *Angst*. Can it be the case that we human beings experience *Angst* as a consequence of our own being? Is what we are "anxious about" genuinely outside of our experience? This beyond-our-experience aspect of our existence is defined neither as an object nor a defined state of affairs. This is what makes the intentional object of our *Angst* maximally quasi-intentional: in *Angst* we intend what escapes us, eluding both cognition's grasp and volition's will.

There is historical justification for seeing Heidegger's view of *Angst* as pre-religious. John van Buren has documented the case that Heidegger, who taught Lutheran theology in his early years at the University of Marburg, "planned to illuminate ontology through his phenomenology of religion" in which he derived his understanding of care from the New Testament interpreted under Luther's *theologia crucis*. "In its widest sense," Heidegger wrote, "the relational meaning of life is: anxiously caring for one's 'daily bread.'" According to van Buren, in a course taught in 1920–21, Heidegger pointed out how "this care is defined through a particular type of understanding, mood, and discourse."[126] In light of his posthumously published comment in *Der Spiegel* that "only a God can

124. See Ibid., 175: "What *Angst* is anxious for is being-in-the-world itself."
125. Ibid., 255.
126. See van Buren, "Martin Heidegger, Martin Luther," 159–74, esp. 162.

save us," perhaps we can acknowledge not only the theological antecedents of Heidegger's philosophy of mood, but also his apologetic intent, if you will, in developing a nontheological philosophy of *Angst*.

In the *philosophy* of this mood, the phenomenon of *Angst* is *inquietum* or unsettledness; nothing more or less. If we wish to find more in *Angst*, we can plausibly think about *Angst* as evidence of our fundamental alienation from one another, from God, and from our own being. But in order for there to be a verification on empirically rigorous grounds, the first thing to say is that *Angst* cannot solely be the product of individual cognition or volition. It is relational in its essence. As a prime datum, it is available to cognitive appraisals. But no cognitive appraisal authorizes us to dismiss the phenomenon as though its purpose is exhausted when its meaning is known. No, its role in consciousness is to continue to unsettle and disquiet us, beyond all knowing.

Here, too, Heidegger sounds the alarm not to sidestep the intentionality of *Angst* in such a way as to make this utterly disconcerting feeling somewhat comfortable for ourselves: "[T]here is in this anxiety an inability to break free of oneself, a final perseverance of the I in itself. In conscience death steps within the horizon of the I, but only as an entity, as an event that conscience can conquer. Human beings think themselves immortal and remain alone."[127] Thus another horizon is opened up by a reminder of the mood's intentionality.

Bonhoeffer cautions us that "Heidegger's concept of death is metaphysical and utterly insincere, for he includes death in the dialectical process of the spirit ('Dasein') finding itself. Inasmuch as 'being towards death' is for him an ontological structure of Dasein, rather than an ontic-existentiell experience, death has already been incorporated into living Dasein."[128] Bonhoeffer's caution is perhaps theologically appropriate, but he has not read Heidegger as closely as one ought, as we can see from the preceding Heidegger passage. Heidegger knows the danger of restricting the field of investigation. He is quite deliberate in analyzing the potential for our contemplation of *Angst* to open to us one horizon after another, by virtue of its intentionality.

In summary, then, our feeling *Angst* toward the world that we inhabit for the time being, which we experience without first thinking or willing this phenomenon, utterly unsettles us. As a feeling, *Angst* cannot

127. Heidegger, *Act and Being*, 148.
128. Ibid., 148 n. 15.

be invalidated, for it is as immediate in its intentionality as it is irrefragable. It is a prime datum for us as human beings. Thus *Angst* validates our situation as individuals whose hearts are disquieted. But *Angst* has more than cognitive content, nor is its own intentionality anything cognitive. So, as to whether this situation is epilogue or prologue for us, that is, as to whether we are irredeemably *inquietum in cor nostrum* or whether this is antecedent to a *requiescat* for us human beings—this remains a matter of gaining more human experience, as Wittgenstein would say, of living and saying, of looking and showing what we feel in the hurly-burly of our engagement with others in the dynamic *Lebensform* of the world.

Appendix: The Argument

STIPULATIONS AND ARGUMENT

I STIPULATE PROFESSOR TALLON's philosophy of triune consciousness argued in his 1997 *Head and Heart: Affection, Cognition, Volition as Triune Consciousness*. That is, I understand affection as an aspect of consciousness that is not reducible either to volition or cognition. I particularly resist the reduction of our basic and higher emotions as well as our moods to cognitions. That said, I view my book as an original contribution to Tallon's project regarding affective intentionality. Whereas, as his index indicates, he addresses affective neuroscience only in a very cursory manner, the support of affective neuroscience to the study of affective intentionality is central to my thesis.

I stipulate the neurological data and the interpretations of the neurology of anxiety in Jaak Panksepp's 1998 *Affective Neuroscience: The Foundations of Human and Animal Emotions*. That said, I view my book as a coherent philosophical response to Panksepp's careful observation that "the abundance of animal models, and the clinical complexity of anxiety indicate that we should be cautious in simplifying the issues that confront us as we seek a definitive understanding of anxiety *within* the mammalian brain."[1]

CHAPTER ONE

The phenomenon of feeling *Angst* is disclosed in Heidegger's existential analysis of conscience as a structural (*struere*, to build upon) feature of human being.

By disclosing the phenomenon of *Angst* in this existential and phenomenological manner, Heidegger brings to light an implicit, abbreviated field theory of emotion.

---

1. Panksepp, *Affective Neuroscience*, 212.

Heidegger defines feeling as "the way we find ourselves in relationship to beings, and thereby at the same time to ourselves." This is at least an implicit, abbreviated field theory of consciousness. Thirty years ago, Bernard Lonergan argued for the scientific worth of what he called "the subjective field of common sense." Such a subjective field or pattern of experience that takes account of human subjects in the world in terms of their patterns of experience perceptually, biologically, aesthetically, and intellectually over time—not as relations of things to other things, but as conscious beings relating to one another in a shared environment. This is what I have in mind.

Within this field, *Angst* is recognizable as a mood, that is, as a long-term felt attunement to our (undefined) world as a whole.

This attunement is a pre-cognitive feature of our being in the world as human beings. In this way, *Angst* is validated as a "primordial" aspect of our being human.

In a word, our feeling of *Angst* exhibits *affective intentionality*.

Regarding intentionality: the Heideggerian conscience, inasmuch as it is an existential concept, is prior to any theological or scientific account. In the same way and for the same reason, *Angst* is an *a priori* or primordial phenomenon of being human beings that simultaneously precedes any and every interpretation of its object. What we seek, then, is an understanding of the source or cause of *Angst*. If *Angst* is intentional, then its source is the thing it is *about*. On the other hand, if *Angst* is nonintentional, then its source is not what the mood is about. My thesis is about the validation of *Angst* on the basis of its intentionality. *Angst* is *about* our being-in-the-world as finite beings.

Angst is also differentiated from basic emotions such as fear by the duration of its intentionality. As a long-term affective intentionality, it "brings perdurance" to our lives by virtue of our felt being-in-the-world.

CHAPTER TWO

A basic objection to this prima facie validation of the mood *Angst* is the claim that *Angst* or anxiety is nothing but a complex of basic emotions that can only be studied as what Paul Griffiths in his 1997 *What Emotions Really Are* calls "[neurological] homologies," or affect systems. Affect systems are the neurological substrates that account for basic emotions.

There is a neuroscientific reply to Griffith's demand for the verification by homologies of emotions and moods alike. The neuroscientific data to date do not support the contention that there is a neurological anxiety system. The assumption, then, that our feeling of *Angst* is reducible to complexes of basic emotions begs the question.

Over the past three decades, there have been at least three proposals for the basic substrates for anxiety: (1) nonadrenergic arousal from the locus coeruleus, (2) serotenergic arousal from midbrain raphe cell groups, and (3) a hippocampal-septal behavioral inhibition system. As Panksepp concludes, each of these theories remains controversial to this day. Most serious, from the neuroscientific standpoint, is the *contradictory data* from animals with these areas and systems experimentally damaged. These animals with damage to the brain areas mentioned above can learn to avoid foot shock and continue to exhibit anxious behaviors. This raises the question as to whether we can account for *Angst* in terms of anxiety systems that we locate predominately *within* the mammalian brain. Perhaps, to put the matter more philosophically, it is a question of recognizing not just *a* cause for anxiety, but a more *complete* account of the causes involved. It is a matter of recognizing the supervenience base needed to account for a mood such as our feeling *Angst*.

By hypothesis, this supervenience base is extra-cranial. It is the structure necessary to account for the intentionality of *Angst* is the world or universe as a whole, though it is undefined and not comprehended by us. Hence we feel our relationship toward it anxiously.

The contradictory data for the various proposed anxiety systems suggest that the analysis of a mood such as *Angst* is unlike a basic emotion such as fear in that a full account of the mood requires a significant extra-cranial field, a social field.

By hypothesis, what is needed for the validation of the phenomenon of *Angst* per se is not a theoretical reduction of this feeling but an adequate supervenience base. This validation, to be suitable as a twenty-first century phenomenology, must seek neuroscientific verification.

CHAPTER THREE

On a weak emergentist analysis, such an adequate supervenience base is available if we extend our operational definition of "mind" to "a nexus of brain-body-world" (Rockwell) and seek an "affective neuroscience-plus." In this case, a spatio-temporal field would embrace both of the elements of affective intentionality, namely, the fittedness of our affective neurology for the world, *and* the continuing calibration of our higher emotions and moods with the objective world in which we live our human form of life for the time being.

One objection to my field theory validation of *Angst* is the sort of "analytic" objection voiced by the Wittgenstein scholar Michael Luntley in his 2003 *Wittgenstein: Meaning and Judgment* who claims that moods, being noncognitive, are irrational.

My reply is to agree that moods are not cognitively constructed. But this does not disqualify moods as engagements with the world or even as rational engagements with the world. It is just that moods are a noncognitive form of engagement with the world.

A second objection to my case for validation by affective intentionality is the sort of predominately biological interpretation of our social background promoted by John Searle.

My reply is to challenge Searle's contention that Wittgenstein's background is essentially a projection of our biology. Although Searle tends to portray the background as a projection of the human organism's neurology, Wittgenstein in fact argues for a social background or *Lebensform* in relation to which the human being's feelings are appraised. Seen in this way, the background is objective. It provides "resistance" to the subject's neurology.

In other words, in order to reply to these objections, we need to speak not in what Brothers calls the language of science in order to organize the "folk psychology" of emotions but rather will need to speak in a language of mood.

This meta-language is the emerging discipline of *social* neuroscience. We could think of social neuroscience as "a language of moods."

In the language of social neuroscience, we should be able to validate not merely the presence of a functioning neuroarchitecture that makes us able to feel *Angst* as human beings but our ongoing moody relationship *with our world* that in turn bioforms our neurology, so to speak, thus pursuing this project in philosophy of mind in a manner respectful of our existential sensibilities and appropriate to a twenty-first century phenomenology that must be neuroscientific.

Consider the familiar example of the interdependence of our neurobiology and our social situatedness in the case of language acquisition. Language acquisition involves both (social) imitation and (brain) formation. The social neuroscientist Bruce Wexler observes these two aspects to acquisition of language, "development-shaping social stimulation" and "characteristics of the brain itself." In the first ten years of a person's life, the period during which a child learns to speak and to understand language with ease, there is a "plasticity of neural structures" that, at the end of this first decade, begins to change "so as to maintain the symmetry and parallels *between inner structure and outer reality.*"

So, in this space *between* society and neurology, we begin to see an indication as to where intentionality is located. This empirical mapping of emotional development is what I referred to above as the bioforming of the brain. The point here is that there is not a static, side-by-side symmetry between brain structure and outer reality, but rather that there is a dynamic forming of the brain's structure that is the result both of its inherent plasticity *and* of its temporally extended embodiment *in the world*. In a similar fashion, I am maintaining that emotional intentionality is the result both of our neuron-architecture *and* of our ongoing engagement *in the world*.

WHAT THIS ARGUMENT IS NOT

Although it begins from a serious study of Heidegger's existential analysis of conscience, entailing as it does the prime datum of *Angst*, this book is not a book on Heidegger. Rather, it employs Heidegger's insight that moods have intentionality to argue for a robustly phenomenological, twenty-first century theory of emotion.

Nor is this book even in part a Wittgensteinian, natural language study of emotion and mood. It did begin that way in an initial draft, but my interpretation of Wittgenstein, particularly in the third chapter, is primarily for the purpose of defeating Searle's understanding of Wittgenstein's concept of the background, which is an objection to my field theory of emotion. The problem is that Searle reduces the objective world (the formal object of our anxious intentionality) to our biology. This reduction creates a nonintentional analysis of mood—this from the author of the book *Intentionality*.

Finally, this is not a neuroscientific paper. The neuroscience contained herein is for the most part derivative from Panksepp. I am not a neurologist; I am philosophy professor who is interested in affective neuroscience and social neuroscience for the further credibility it affords our study of affective intentionality. Because of the recent emergence of affective neuroscience and of social neuroscience, this is a preliminary philosophical argument as to how we may validate the intentionality of the mood of *Angst* today.

Glossary

Affect systems: The neurological substrates that account for basic emotions.

Affective neuroscience: The study of physiology, endocrinology, and especially neurology pertinent to emotions, usually in terms of the mammalian brain. Panksepp's *Affective Neuroscience* is the standard reference.

Angst, anguish, anxiety: A *mood* recognizable but not always recognized by the human being in which he irrefragably feels himself to be disquieted, unsettled, and not at home in the world in which he exists for the time being. "The most celebrated mood."[2]

Anxiety systems: Putative neurological explanations of the mood of anxiety, offered on the model of affect systems for *basic emotions*. Candidates for anxiety systems or basic substrates for anxiety to date include: nonadrenergic arousal from the locus coeruleus, serotenergic arousal from midbrain raphe cell groups, and a hippocampal-septal behavioral inhibition system. The data for these candidate anxiety systems are contradictory.

Background: One's social environment. Although Searle tends to portray the Background as a projection of the human organism's biology, Wittgenstein in fact argues for a social background or *Lebensform* in relation to which the human being's feelings are appraised.

Basic emotions: Affects that are common among animals and humans by virtue of the common structural features of the mammalian brain. Griffiths refers to these common structures as "homologous." Although neuroscientists differ in their catalogues of the basic emotions, the emotions of fear and anger are almost universally considered "basic." They are identified as basic emotions on the basis of their common, mammalian

---

2. Tallon, *Head and Heart*, 100.

neurological substrates or *affect systems*, and are essentially autonomic and short-term, in contrast to the so-called higher-level emotions and moods.

Conscience: Heidegger's existential analysis of conscience, in which the prime datum of the mood of *Angst* is disclosed as the basis for responsible individuality, is unlike Aquinas's theological analysis or Kant's rational analysis of conscience. It is pre-theological and pre-scientific in that it presents a basis, namely, the mood *Angst*, for the traditional analyses in the essential or "primordial" disquiet of the human being as *Dasein*.

Emergentist: The emergentist aspect of this argument depends upon the neuroscientific understanding that our brain is both *hierarchical*—the higher or cortical builds on the lower or subcortical—and it is *modular* in that the affective and cognitive do not reduce to one another. This is due, according to Panksepp, to different evolutionary developments, different locations, and different chemistries. It depends as well upon the Heideggerian understanding that we have are *in der Welt sein*. Thus the *supervenience* base from which *Angst* emerges is simultaneously our neurology and our being-in-the-world.

Field theory, behavioral field, field of consciousness: The supervenience base for all mental events, including subjective experiences. It includes, as Rockwell has it, not only brain events but also events in the rest of the body and in those parts of the environment with which the conscious organism maintains a synergetic relationship.

Gefühl: Wittgenstein's term for (both sensory and emotional) feeling. In his *Nietzsche* lectures, Heidegger defines a feeling as an "openness to being," one's own and the being of others. A feeling is never merely subjective (compare Wittgenstein's private language argument) but is best "located" in the public space-time of our social intercourse.

Intentionality: That a feeling, emotion, or mood is *about* something; its objectivity. A mood such as *Angst* is *about* the world as a whole, the undefined world in which an individual is situated. This situatedness is immediate and is not reducible either to cognition or volition. The "location" of intentionality is best understood as a spatio-temporal field of consciousness and intersubjective experience.

Language of mind: A manner of speaking of affects, emotions, and moods that is concerned with conceptual analysis. This is the type of *validation* in which phenomenologists and existentialists such as Heidegger are typically engaged. Language of mind theorists do not, as a rule, seek neuroscientific *verification.*

Language of mood: A manner of speaking of moods such as *Angst* that is neuroscientific but also attentive to affective intentionality. A language of mood respects Heidegger's insight that moods too (and not only cognitions) have intentionality while simultaneously seeking empirical evidence for this in *social neuroscience.*

Language of science: A manner of speaking of affect programs and basic emotions that is concerned with neurological imaging. This is the type of *verification* in which neuroscientists such as Panksepp and researchers such as Griffiths are typically engaged. Neuroscientists prefer "nothing-but theories"[3] regarding higher-level emotions and moods, in order to pursue *verification* predominately within the (brain of the) organism with minimal attention to its dynamic concourse with its environment.

Mind: Once considered to be coextensive with "brain" and then with "brain and body," this term is best construed, for example, as in Rockwell, as a nexus of brain-body-world in which there is a fluid boundary between the human being and the world.

Mood: A long-term, immediate, and irreducible intentionality that has as its formal object the world as a whole. Although moods have a neurological component or substrate, they are best studied scientifically "in terms of a field theory that can account for events in the rest of the body and in those parts of the environment with which the conscious organism maintains a synergetic relationship."[4] Moods discussed by twentieth-century philosophers such as Heidegger and Wittgenstein include anguish or anxiety, joy, and equanimity. See Bollnow as well for a sustained argument that moods, rather than cognitions, are primary to human being.

---

3. Searle, *Mind, Language, and Society,* 47.
4. Rockwell, *Neither Brain Nor Ghost,* 206.

Social neuroscience: An emerging neuroscience that studies the brain in light of the presumably substantial influence of environment on brain development and processes. Brothers, Rockwell, and Wexler are noteworthy contributors to *social* neuroscience.

Umwelt: One's environment, not in the sense of proximate objects, but in the sense of that which one *cares* about.

Validation: A way of securing the rational role and thus the human worth of emotions and moods by conceptual analysis. This is usually the goal of theorists of emotion who espouse what Brothers calls "the *language of the mind.*" By hypothesis, a twenty-first century validation of a mood ought to entail as well scientific *verification.*

Verification: A way of investigating the nature of emotions and moods by scientific methodologies. This is usually associated with theorists of emotion who espouse what Brothers calls "the *language of science.*" By hypothesis, current methods for verifying basic emotions are insufficient for verifying *moods.* For this reason, a neuroscience of *moods* can benefit from the conceptual insights of philosophers who have articulated the intentionality of *Angst,* joy, and equanimity, for example.

Weak supervenience: In relation to traditional neuroscience, the present theory is "weak" insofar as the brain and its neurophysiological processes are regarded as necessary but not sufficient conditions to account for higher emotions and *moods* such as *Angst.* The sufficient conditions needed to account for the human phenomenon of feeling *Angst*—which may also be called "the supervenience base"—extend beyond the cranium into the world as a whole (see *field theory* above).

Bibliography

Anscombe, G. E. M., and G. H. von Wright. *Ludwig Wittgenstein: Zettel.* Berkeley and Los Angeles: University of California Press, 1970.
Augustine. *Confessions.* Cambridge, MA: Harvard University Press, 1996.
Barbiero, Daniel. "The Background." In *Dictionary of Philosophy of Mind.* No pages. Online: http://www.philosophy.uwaterloo.ca/MindDict.
Bonhoeffer, Dietrich. *Ethics.* New York: Simon and Schuster, 1995.
Becchio, Christina, and Cesare Bertone. "Wittgenstein Running: Neural Mechanisms of Collective Intentionality and We-Mode." *Consciousness and Cognition* 13 (2004) 123–33.
Bishop, DVM. "Linguistic Impairment after Left Hemidecortication for Infantile Hemiplegia? A Reappraisal." *The Quarterly Journal of Experimental Psychology* 35A (1983) 199–208.
Bollnow, Otto Friedrich. *Des Wegen der Stimmungen.* Frankfurt am Main: Vittorio Klostermann, 1995. My understanding of Bollnow is based upon personal correspondence from Andrew Tallon (April–May 2006).
Brock, Werner. *Martin Heidegger: Existence and Being.* South Bend, IN: Regnery/Gateway, 1979.
Brothers, Leslie. *Friday's Footprint: How Society Shapes the Human Mind.* New York: Oxford University Press, 1997.
———. *Mistaken Identity: The Mind-Brain Problem Reconsidered.* New York: SUNY Press, 2001.
Caygill, Howard. "Conscience." In *A Kant Dictionary*, edited by Howard Caygill, 204–5. Malden, MA: Blackwell, 1995.
Caputo, John. "*Sorge* and *Kardia*: The Hermeneutics of Factical Life and the Categories of the Heart." In *Reading Heidegger from the Start: Essays in His Earliest Thought*, edited by Theodore Kisiel and John van Buren, 327–44. New York: SUNY Press, 1994.
Carman, Taylor. *Heidegger's Analytic: Interpretation, Discourse, and Authenticity in Being and Time.* Cambridge, UK: Cambridge University Press, 2003.
Chalier, Catherine. *What Ought I to Do? Morality in Kant and Levinas.* Translated by Jane Mary Todd. Ithaca, NY: Cornell University Press, 2002.
Chouchourelou, Arieta, et al. "The Visual Analysis of Emotional Actions." *Social Neuroscience* Vol. 1, No. 1 (2006) 63–74.
Damasio, Antonio. *Descartes' Error: Emotion, Reason, and the Human Brain.* New York: HarperCollins and Avon, 1994.
———. *The Feeling of What Happens: Body and Emotion in the Making of Consciousness.* New York: Harcourt, 1999.
———. *Looking for Spinoza: Joy, Sorrow and the Feeling Brain.* New York: Harcourt, 2003.

DeLancey, Craig. *Passionate Engines: What Emotions Reveal about Mind and Artificial Intelligence.* New York: Oxford University Press, 2002.

Del Nevo, Matthew. "What Exactly Is Feeling Then, According to Heidegger?" No pages. Online: http://www.sicetnon.com.

Dennett, Daniel. "*Quining Qualia.*" In *Consciousness in Modern Science,* edited by A. Marcel and E. Bisiach, 42–58. New York: Oxford University Press, 1988.

de Sousa, Ronald. "Emotional Truth." *Proceedings of the Aristotelean Society, Supplement* 76 (July 2002) 247–63.

———. "Emotion." In *The Stanford Encyclopedia of Philosophy,* edited by Edward N. Zalta. Spring 2003 edition. No pages. Online: http://plato.stanford.edu/archives/spr2003/entries/emotion.

Dennett, Daniel. *Consciousness Explained.* New York: Little, Brown and Company, 1991.

———. *The Intentional Stance.* Cambridge, MA: MIT Press, 1989.

Dowling, John. *The Retina, an Approachable Part of the Brain.* Cambridge, UK: Belknapp, 1987.

Dreyfus, Hubert. "Intelligence without Representation." No pages. Online: http://www.hfac.uh.edu/cogsci/dreyfus.html.

Eliot, T. S. *The Complete Poems and Plays, 1909–1950.* New York: Harcourt, Brace Jovanovich, 1971.

Gadamer, Hans-Georg. "Martin Heidegger's One Path." In *Reading Heidegger from the Start: Essays in His Earliest Thought,* edited by Theodore Kisiel and John van Buren, translated by P. Christopher Smith, 19–34. New York: SUNY Press, 1994.

Gendlin, Eugene. "*Befindlichkeit*: Heidegger and the Philosophy of Psychology." *Review of Existential Psychology and Psychiatry: Heidegger and Psychology* Vol. XVI, Nos. 1, 2, and 3 (1978–1979) 43–78.

Gluck, Hans-Johann. *A Wittgenstein Dictionary.* Oxford, UK: Blackwell, 1996.

Gloor, Pierre. "The Role of the Human Limbic System in Perception, Memory, and Affect: Lessons from Temporal Lobe Epilepsy." In *The Limbic System: Functional Organization and Clinical Disorders,* edited by Benjamin K. Doane and Kenneth E. Livingston, 159–69. New York: Raven, 1986.

Goldie, Peter. "Emotion, Feeling, and Knowledge of the World." In *Thinking about Feeling: Contemporary Philosophers on Emotions,* edited by Robert Solomon, 91–106. Oxford, UK: Oxford University Press, 2004.

———. "Narrative and Perspective; Values and Appropriate Emotions" In *Philosophy and the Emotions,* edited by Anthony Hatzimoysis, 201–20. Cambridge, UK: Cambridge University Press, 2003.

Graeff, Fred, Stella Quintero, and Jeffrey A. Gray. "Median Raphe Stimulation, Hippocampal Theta Rhythm and Threat-Induced Behavioral Inhibition." *Physiology and Behavior* 25:253 (1980) 2–61.

Gray, Jeffrey A., and Neil McNaughton. *The Neuropsychology of Anxiety: An Enquiry into the Function of the Septo-Hippocampal System.* Oxford, UK: Oxford University Press, 1982.

Gregor, Mary. *The Cambridge Edition of the Works of Immanuel Kant: Practical Philosophy.* Translated by Mary Gregor. New York: Cambridge University Press, 1996.

Griffiths, Paul. *What Emotions Really Are: The Problem of Psychological Categories.* Chicago: University of Chicago Press, 1997.

———. "Emotions as Natural Kinds." In *Thinking about Feeling: Contemporary Philosophers on Emotion*, edited by Robert Solomon, 233–49. New York: Oxford University Press, 2004.

———. "Basic Emotions, Complex Emotions, Machiavellian Emotions." In *Philosophy and the Emotions*, edited by Anthony Hatzimoysis, 39–68. Cambridge: Cambridge University Press, 2003.

Grondin, Jean. "*Das junhegelianische und ethische Motiv in Heideggers Hermenteutic der Faktizitaet*" as "The Ethical and Young Hegelian Motives in Heidegger's Hermeneutics of Facticity." In *Reading Heidegger from the Start: Essays in His Earliest Thought*, edited by Theodore Kisiel and John van Buren, 348. Albany, New York: SUNY Press, 1994.

Heidegger, Martin. *Being and Time*. Translated by Joan Stambaugh. New York: State University of New York Press, 1996.

———. *Being and Time*. Translated by Macquarrie and Robinson. New York: Harper and Row, 1962.

———. "Rapture as Aesthetic State." In *Nietzsche*, Volume One, edited and translated by David Farrell Krell, 92–106. San Francisco: HarperSanFrancisco, 1991.

———. "Will as Affect, Passion, and Feeling," In *Nietzsche*, Volume One, edited and translated by David Farrell Krell, 44–53. San Francisco: HarperSanFrancisco, 1991.

Hoffmann, Piotr. "Death, Time, History: Division II of *Being and Time*." In *The Cambridge Companion to Heidegger*, edited by Charles P. Guignon, 195–214. New York: Cambridge University Press, 1999.

Horgan, John. *The Undiscovered Mind: How the Human Brain Defies Replication, Medication, and Explanation*. New York: Touchstone, 2000.

Husserl, Edmund. *Ideas: General Introduction to Pure Phenomenology*. Translated by W. R. Boyce Gibson. New York: Macmillan, 1931. German edition *Ideen zu einer reinen Phänomenologie und phänomenologischen Philosophie*. Vol. I. Halle, Germany: Niemeyer, 1913.

Inwood, Michael. "Conscience and Guilt." In *A Heidegger Dictionary*, edited by Michael J. Inwood, 37–39. Malden, MA: Blackwell, 2000.

Irvine, William. *On Desire: Why We Want What We Want*. New York: Oxford University Press, 2006.

Jaspers, Karl. *Nietzsche: An Introduction to the Study of His Philosophical Activity*. Translated by Charles Wallraff and Frederick Schmitz. Baltimore: Johns Hopkins University Press, 1997.

Johannson, Ingvar. *Ontological Investigations: An Inquiry into the Categories of Nature, Man and Society*. London: Routledge, 1989.

Johnston, William. *The Cloud of Unknowing and the Book of Privy Counseling*. New York: Doubleday, 2005.

Kant, Immanuel. *Anthropology from a Pragmatic Point of View*. Translated by Victor Dowdell. Edwardsville, IL: Southern Illinois University Press, 1978.

Kim, Jaegwon. *Mind in a Physical World: An Essay on the Mind-Body Problem and Mental Causation*. Cambridge, MA: MIT Press, 2000.

King, Magda. "Witness to an Owned Existence and Authentic Resolution." In *A Guide to Heidegger's Being and Time*, edited by John Llewelyn, 163–200. Albany, NY: State New York University Press, 2001.

Peter Kramer, *Listening to Prozac*. New York: Penguin, 1997.

Bibliography

Krebs, Victor. "Mind, Soul, Language in Wittgenstein." In *Paideia*. No pages. Online: www.bu.edu/ wcp/Papers/Lang/LangKreb.htm.

Lakoff, George, and Mark Johnson. *Philosophy in the Flesh: The Embodied Mind and Its Challenge to Western Thought*. New York: Basic Books, 1999.

Lem, Stanislaw. *Solaris*. Translated by Johanna Kilmartin and Steve Cox. New York: Faber and Faber, 1970.

Levinas, Emmanuel. *Ethics and Infinity*. Pittsburgh: Duquesne University Press, 1985.

———. *Otherwise than Being or Beyond Essence*. Translated by Alphonso Lingis. The Hague: Nijhoff, 1981.

———. *Totality and Infinity: An Essay on Exteriority*. Translated by Alphonso Lingis. Pittsburgh: Duquesne University Press, 1969.

Lonergan, Bernard. *Insight: A Study of Human Understanding*. New York: Harper & Row, 1978.

Luntley, Michael. *Wittgenstein: Meaning and Judgment*. Oxford, UK: Blackwell, 2003.

Macquarrie, John. *Heidegger and Christianity: The Hensley Lectures, 1993–94*. New York: Continuum, 1999.

Magee, Bryan. *The Great Philosophers: An Introduction to Western Philosophy*. Oxford, UK: Oxford University Press, 1988.

McDermott, Timothy. *St. Thomas Aquinas' Summa Theologiae: A Concise Translation*. Westminster, MD: Christian Classics, 1989.

McGinn, Colin. "Searle: Contract with Reality." In *Minds and Bodies: Philosophers and Their Ideas*, edited by Colin McGinn, 191–96. Oxford, UK: Oxford University Press, 1997.

Meinong, Alexius. *On Emotional Presentation*. Translated by Marie-Luise Schubert Kalsi. Evanston, IL: Northwestern University Press, 1972.

Merleau-Ponty, Maurice. *The Primacy of Perception*. Translated by James M. Edie. Evanston, IL: Northwestern University Press, 1964.

———. *The Structure of Behavior*. Translated by Alden L. Fischer. Boston: Beacon, 1963.

———. "An Unpublished Text by Merleau-Ponty: A Prospectus of His Work." Translated by Arleen B. Dallery. In *The Primacy of Perception and Other Essays on Phenomenological Psychology*, edited by James Edie, 3–11. Evanston, IL: Northwestern University Press, 1964.

Namely, Kinsbourne. "The Minor Cerebral Hemisphere as a Source of Aphasic Speech." *Archives of Neurology* 25 (1971) 302–6.

Natanson, Maurice, *Edmund Husserl: Philosopher of Infinite Tasks*. Evanston, IL: Northwestern University Press, 1973.

Nussbaum, Martha. *Upheavals of Thought: The Intelligence of Emotions*. Cambridge, UK: Cambridge University Press, 2001.

Panksepp, Jaak. *Affective Neuroscience: The Foundations of Human and Animal Emotions*. New York: Oxford University Press, 1998.

Polt, Richard. *Heidegger: An Introduction*. Ithaca, NY: Cornell University Press, 1999.

Popkin, Richard. *The Columbia History of Western Philosophy*. New York: MJF Books, 1999.

Redmond, D. Eugene, and Yinghua Huang. "New Evidence for a Locus Coeruleus Norepinephrine Connection with Anxiety." *Life Science*. 25 (1979) 2149–62.

Robins, Brent. "Review of Griffith's *Griffiths, What Emotions Really Are*." No pages. Online: http://mentalhelp.net, 2001.

Rockwell, W. Teed. *Neither Brain Nor Ghost: A Non-Dualist Alternative to the Mind-Brain Identity Theory.* Cambridge, MA: MIT Press, 2005.

Rose, Steven, Richard Lewontin, and Leon Kamin,. *Biology, Ideology and Human Nature.* New York: Penguin, 1984.

Sartre, Jean Paul. *Being and Nothingness: An Essay on Phenomenological Ontology.* Translated by Hazel Barnes. New York: Philosophical Library, 1956.

Schacht, Richard. *Making Sense of Nietzsche: Reflections Timely and Untimely.* Urbana, IL: University of Illinois Press, 1995.

Schulz, Gregory. "David Bloor: *Wittgenstein: Rules and Institutions*" (review). *Dialogue* 74 (2004) 37–38.

———. "A Non-Traditional Analysis of Conscience: The Place of Conscience in *Being and Time.*" *De Philosophia* 19 (2006) 33–34.

Shackman, Alexander, et al. "Anxiety Selectively Disrupts Visuaspatial Working Memory." *Emotion* Vol. 6, No. 1 (2006) 40–61.

Searle, John. *Consciousness Explained.* Boston: Little, Brown, and Company, 1991.

———. *The Construction of Social Reality.* New York: Free Press, 1995.

———. *Intentionality: An Essay in the Philosophy of Mind.* Cambridge, UK: Cambridge University Press, 1983.

———. *Mind, Language, and Society: Philosophy in the Real World.* New York: Basic Books, 1998.

———. *The Rediscovery of the Mind.* Cambridge, MA: MIT Press, 1992.

Smith, Quentin. "On Heidegger's Theory of Moods." *The Modern Schoolman: A Quarterly Journal in Philosophy* Vol. LVIII, number 4 (1981) 211–35.

Solomon, Robert. "Are Emotions 'in' the Mind?" A lecture in the *series The Passions: Philosophy and the Intelligence of Emotions.* Chantilly, VA: The Learning Company, 2006.

———. "Emotions, Thoughts and Feelings: Emotions as Engagements with the World." In *Thinking about Feeling: Contemporary Philosophers on Emotions,* edited by Robert Solomon, 76–90. New York: Oxford University Press, 2004.

———. "Emotions, Thoughts and Feelings: What is a 'Cognitive Theory' of the Emotions and Does it Neglect Affectivity?" In *Philosophy and the Emotions,* edited by Anthony Hatzimoysis, 1–18. Cambridge, UK: Cambridge University Press, 2003.

———. *Philosophy and the Intelligence of Emotions.* Chantilly, VA: The Learning Company, 2006.

Stableford, Brian. *The Dictionary of Science Fiction Places.* New York: Simon and Schuster, 1999.

Stanovich, Keith. *The Robot's Rebellion: Finding Meaning in the Age of Darwin.* Chicago: University of Chicago Press, 2004.

Stambaugh, Joan. *The Real is not the Rational.* New York: SUNY Press, 1986.

Stone, Valerie, et al. "Selective Impairment of Social Inferences Following Orbitofrontal Cortex Damage." In *Proceedings of the Cognitive Science Society,* Vol. 99, No. 1, edited by Michael Shaft and Pat Langley, 11,531–36. Mahway, New Jersey: Cognitive Science Society, August 2, 2002.

Tallon, Andrew. *Head and Heart: Affection, Cognition, Volition as Triune Consciousness.* New York: Fordham University Press, 1997.

Taminiaux, Jacques. *The Metamorphoses of Phenomenological Reduction.* Milwaukee: Marquette University Press, 2004.

Taylor, Charles. "Lichtung or Lebensform: Parallels between Heidegger and Wittgenstein." In his *Philosophical Arguments*, 61–78. Cambridge, MA: Harvard University Press, 1997.

Thornton, Tim. *Wittgenstein on Language and Thought: The Philosophy of Content*. Edinburgh: Edinburgh University Press, 1998.

van Buren, John. "Martin Heidegger, Martin Luther." In *Reading Heidegger from the Start: Essays in His Earliest Thought*, edited by Theodore Kisiel and John van Buren, 159–74. Albany, NY: SUNY Press, 1994.

Wexler, Bruce. *Brain and Culture: Neurobiology, Ideology, and Social Change*. Cambridge, MA: MIT Press, 2006.

Wittgenstein, Ludwig. *Philosophical Investigations*. 1999 German-English edition. Translated by G. E. M. Anscombe. Malden, MA: Blackwell, 1953.

———. *On Certainty*. Edited by G. E. M. Anscombe and G. H. von Wright. Oxford, UK: Blackwell, 1969.

———. *Culture and Value*. Edited by G. H. von Wright. Oxford, UK: Blackwell, 1980.

———. *Remarks on the Philosophy of Psychology*. Translated by G. H. von Wright and H. Nyman. Chicago: University of Chicago Press, 1980.

———. *Tractatus Logico-Philosophicus*. German-English version. Translated by G. K. Ogden. London: Routledge, 2002.

———. *Zettel*. Edited by G. E. M. Anscombe and G.H. von Wright, translated by G. E. M. Anscombe. Berkeley: University of California Press, 1970.

Zaidel, Eran. "Language in the Right Hemisphere." In *The Dual Brain*, edited by D. Frank Benson and Eran Zaidel, 205–32. New York: Guilford Press, 1985.

www.ingramcontent.com/pod-product-compliance
Lightning Source LLC
Chambersburg PA
CBHW071857160426
43197CB00013B/2518